Contents

UNIT 1 — START LOCAL – THINK GLOBAL   1

UNIT 2 — CHANGING LANDSCAPE   21

UNIT 3 — SETTLEMENT   43

UNIT 4 WEATHER AND CLIMATE 65

UNIT 5 FARMING 87

UNIT 6 FRANCE 109

earth

1

John Widdowson

11–14
GEOGRAPHY
PROJECT

JOHN MURRAY

© John Widdowson 1998

First published 1998
by John Murray (Publishers) Ltd
50 Albemarle Street
London W1X 4BD

Reprinted 1999

Artwork by Countryside Illustrations, David Farris, Hardlines, Janek Matysiak, Steve Smith
Layouts by Liz Rowe
Cover design by John Townson/Creation
Typeset in 11.5/13pt Sabon by Wearset, Boldon, Tyne and Wear
Printed and bound in Great Britain by Butler and Tanner, Frome and London

A CIP catalogue record for this book is available from the British Library

ISBN 0 7195 7070 0

Teacher's Resource Book ISBN 0 7195 7071 9

Acknowledgements

The author would like to thank the following people, who have all contributed to *Earthworks 1*: Keith Mears, Andy Schofield and Jeff Stanfield for all their helpful ideas and criticism; pupils at Forest Gate School; Sue Earle, Claire Jones and Great Linford Combined School; Hilary Fouweather and the Kendal Mountain Rescue Team; Tom and Eva Cowcher, Virginia Duncanson, Claudine and Patrick Ellis, Alain Viélmas, Bernardette Van Accoleyen and Jean and Jeanine Raynier.

The publishers gratefully acknowledge the contribution made by the following sources.

Maps on **pp. 7, 31, and 56** reproduced from the Ordnance Survey mapping with permission of the Controller of Her Majesty's Stationery Office © Crown Copyright Licence Number 399604.
Maps on **pp. 8, 19 and 127** © Collins-Longman Atlases.
Map on **p.60** reproduced with permission of GEOprojects Ltd.
Map on **p.122** © Michelin from Map 235, 16th Edition, 1997/98 Authorization no. 9802084.
Article on **p.130** reproduced with permission from the *Guardian*.

Photo credits

Cover: *bl* European Space Agency/Science Photo Library, *br* Richard Greenhill/Sally & Richard Greenhill, *remainder* ZEFA; **p.iii** *t* ESA/PLI/Science Photo Library, *c* Landform Slides, *b* © Crispin Hughes/Photofusion; **p.iv** *t* Tim Cuff/Apex, *c* Peter Menzel/Science Photo Library; **p.1** ESA/ PLI/Science Photo Library; **p.2** *b* © David Simson; **p.3** *tl* ESA/PLI/Science Photo Library, *cl* Photoair Ltd, *cr & bl* M-Sat Ltd/Science Photo Library; **p.10** Photoair Ltd; **p.13** *bl & br* Sally & Richard Greenhill; **p.17** *tl & br* Jeanetta Baker/International Photobank, *tr* Peter Baker/International Photobank, *bl* © Trip/J. Short; **p.18** *tl* Geoscience Features Picture Library, *tr* Alex Gillespie/The Edinburgh Photographic Library, *bl* © Doug Allan/Oxford Scientific Films, *br* O. Vitale/Small Print; **p.21** Landform Slides; **p.22** *all* Prodeepta Das; **p.23** *both* Prodeepta Das; **p.24** *tl* Landform Slides, *tr* Collections/Gary Smith, *bl* Martin Bond/Science Photo Library, *br* Mr Jules Cowan/Bruce Coleman Limited; **p.28** Rex Features; **p.29** Scarborough Borough Council; **p.33** *both* © Trip/H. Rogers; **p.34** *both* © Trip/H. Rogers; **p.35** Collections/Michael Allen; **p.37** Aerofilms; **p.40** *both* Popperfoto; **p.41** Alex Bartel/Science Photo Library; **p.42** *t* © Sealand Aerial Photography, *b* © Trip/J. Ringland; **p.43** © Crispin Hughes/Photofusion; **p.44** *t* © Yorkshire Television Ltd, *b* © BBC; **p.45** © Grundy Television. A Pearson Television Company; **p.47** *all* Jason Hawkes Aerial Collection/Julian Cotton Photo Library; **p.49** *t* Aerofilms, *c & b* courtesy East Riding of Yorkshire Council; **p.51** Collections/Peter Wright; **p.53** *tl* Collections/Eamonn McNulty, *tr* Collections/Brian Shuel, *bl* Collections/Liz Stares, *br* © Santiago Castrillon/ Photofusion; **p.54** *t* Pushkin Museum, Moscow/Bridgeman Art Library, London, *b* Collections/Alain Le Garsmeaur; **p.57** *both* © Trip/G. Horner; **p.58** *r* © Sealand Aerial Photography; **p.62** Popperfoto; **p.63** *t* Rex Features, *b* Alexandre Tokitaka/SIPA Press/Rex Features; **p.65** Tim Cuff/Apex; **p.66** *t* David Ducros/Science Photo Library, *b* Today/Rex Features; **p.67** *tl* Ecoscene/Quentin Bates, *tr* Popperfoto, *b* © George Montgomery/Photofusion; **p.68** Cape Grim B.A.P.S./Simon Fraser/Science Photo Library; **p.70** *t* © Martyn Colback/Oxford Scientific Films, *b* © Niall Benvie/Oxford Scientific Films; **p.73** *t* Collections/ Robert Hallmann, *b* © C. Stadtler/Photofusion; **p.74** *both* Vincent Lowe; **p.75** *both* Vincent Lowe; **p.76** *tl & r* Vincent Lowe, *bl* © Vincent Lowe/Kendal Mountain Rescue Team; **p.80** *tl* Bord Failte (Irish Tourist Board) Photo, *tr* The Stock Market, *ct* Charles Knight/Rex Features, *cb* © Trip/Colin Baker, *b* © David Simson; **p.83** *t* Staffan Widstrand/Bruce Coleman Limited, *b* Sinclair Stammers/Science Photo Library; **p.84** NRSC Ltd/Science Photo Library; **p.85** *l* John Mead/Science Photo Library, *r* Pekka Parviainen/Science Photo Library; **p.86** Rex Features; **p.87** Peter Menzel/Science Photo Library; **p.88** © Sally & Richard Greenhill; **p.89** © Trip/D. Davis; **p.90** *t* Bob Gibbons/Holt Studios, *cl* Public Record Office Image Library, *cr* Quentin Bates/Ecoscene, *b* Gordon Roberts/Holt Studios; **p.91** *t* Maximilian Stock Ltd/Science Photo Library, *c* James Holmes/Reed Nurse/Science Photo Library, *b* John Heseltine/Science Photo Library; **p.92** *t* Rural History Centre, University of Reading, *b* Nigel Cattlin/Holt Studios; **p.95** *t* Miss P. Peacock/Holt Studios, *b* © Farmer's Weekly Picture Library; **p.100** *tl* David Burton/Holt Studios, *tr & c* Nigel Cattlin/Holt Studios, *bl* © Farmer's Weekly Picture Library, *bc* © Trip/D. Turner, *br* © John Watt/The Edinburgh Photographic Library; **p.102** *t* Nigel Cattlin/Holt Studios, *b* John Townson/Creation; **p.104** Nigel Cattlin/Holt Studios; **p.105** *tr* Bob Gibbons/Holt Studios; **p.106** Nigel Cattlin/Holt Studios; **p.107** *both* John Townson/Creation; **p.109** *tr* Daniel Valla/Survival Anglia/Oxford Scientific Films, *bl* Roy Handford/ Survival Anglia/Oxford Scientific Films, *br* © Christer Fredriksson/ Bruce Coleman Limited; **p.111** *tr* Daniel Valla/Survival Anglia/Oxford Scientific Films, *bl* Roy Handford/Survival Anglia/Oxford Scientific Films, *br* © Christer Fredriksson/Bruce Coleman Limited; **p.112** *t & br* © David Simson; **p.115** *tl* The Stock Market, *tr & br* Julian Cotton Photo Library, *bl* © Trip/B. Gadsby; **p.124** *br* © Trip/T. Bognar; **p.128** *t* © Harlingue-Viollet, *b* © Trip/H. Rogers.

All other photos supplied by the author.

b = bottom, *c* = centre, *l* = left, *r* = right, *t* = top.

Every effort has been made to trace all copyright holders, but if any have been inadvertently overlooked the publishers will be pleased to make the necessary arrangement at the first opportunity.

About Earthworks

In *Earthworks 1* there are six units. Each unit covers a different geographical theme, or country. You will notice that the units follow a similar pattern, and have the same features.

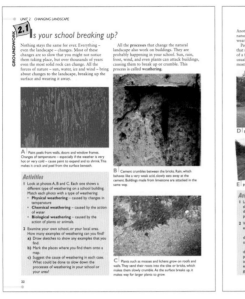

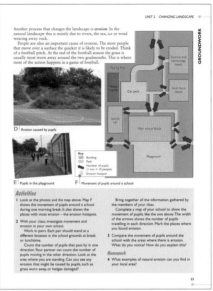

GROUNDWORK – an introduction to the unit, based on your everyday experience of geography.

Activities

You can do most of these in your class, either on your own, or in a group. They often involve writing or drawing, but looking and thinking are important activities too.

FRAMEWORK – covers all the key geographical ideas which you need to understand in that unit.

Key words

New geographical words are printed in **bold** letters. These are words you really need to know. The glossary at the back of the book includes these words, and tells you their meanings. You will probably find it helpful to keep your own dictionary of these words as you go through the book.

Homework

This is an activity that you could do at home. It often involves doing some extra research on your own.

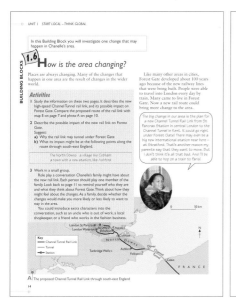

BUILDING BLOCKS – two or three geographical investigations, based on the *Framework* ideas, using real places.

Local investigation

These are investigations which you can do with the rest of your class in your own local area, or as part of a geography field trip.

These show the best opportunities to use a computer to help you with the activities you do. But they are not the only opportunities. There are many ways that computers can help you to do geography.

DIGGING DEEPER – an in-depth look at a topical issue, to take your geography that little bit further.

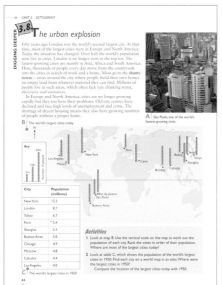

Assignment

This is an extended activity where you are expected to use many of the geographical skills and ideas from the unit.

UNIT 1 START LOCAL – THINK GLOBAL

The Earth photographed from a satellite in space

Geography is about the Earth, the places on it and the people who live there.

- Can you see the place where you live?
- Which other parts of the world can you see?
- What can you find out about those places from the photo?
- Which parts of the world can't you see in the photo?
- Why can't you see the whole world?

GROUNDWORK

1.1 Where do you live?

You are already a geography expert! You have been learning about the world around you from the day you were born. You know more about your local area than the person who wrote this book. In geography you will learn even more about the world than you already know.

One of the best ways to learn in geography is to ask questions. You will notice many questions throughout this book. These questions are the sort of things you might want to know about a place: Where is it?, What is it like?, How did it get like this?, How is it changing? and Why? You may think of many other questions. Don't be afraid to ask!

In this unit you will investigate a local area through maps and photos. You will think of questions to ask about it. You can also do this in your own area.

Activities

1 Look at the photos on the opposite page. What places do they show? Match each photo (except F) with one of the words in the box.

> street planet city
> country home continent
> local area

2 The photos don't show the real size of each place. For example, a country is usually much larger than a city.

Sort the places in order of their real size, starting with the smallest.

Use the places you have sorted to write Chanelle's address.

3 Write your own address in full, in the same way.

4 Look at photos A and B, which show homes in other parts of the world. Think of some questions that you would like to ask about them.

A

B

C The world

D Chestnut Avenue

E Forest Gate

F Chanelle

G London

H Europe

I Great Britain

J Number 99

FRAMEWORK

1.2 Geography begins at home

In geography, one of the best ways to show a place is to use a **map**. This is the view from above. It is sometimes called a bird's-eye view. A map can be of a large place, like a country, or a small place, like your street. Maps of small places are called **plans**.

Maps and plans usually have **symbols** and a **key**. Symbols are used to show things that may be hard to recognise from above, or to save space. The key explains what the symbols mean.

Maps and plans show places smaller than they are in real life. To draw a plan accurately, or to measure distance on a plan, you have to use a **scale**. The scale tells you how much smaller the plan is than real life. The **scale line** on Chanelle's bedroom plan (see A) tells you that 4 cm (centimetres) on the plan is 2 metres in real life. This can also be written as a ratio – 1 : 50 (1 cm on the plan is 50 cm in real life).

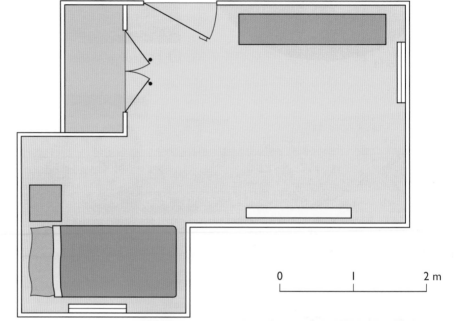

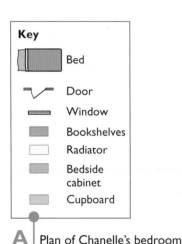

Key

- Bed
- Door
- Window
- Bookshelves
- Radiator
- Bedside cabinet
- Cupboard

0   I   2 m

A | Plan of Chanelle's bedroom

Activities

1 Look at the plan of Chanelle's bedroom. Use the key to understand the symbols on the plan.

2 Look at the photo of Chanelle's bedroom. What things are missing from the plan? Think of symbols that you could use to show them on a plan.
   On a copy of the plan, draw symbols for things that are missing. Add them to the key. Colour the symbols on the plan and in the key.

3 Work out the real size of Chanelle's bedroom, using the scale.
   Work out the real size of each of the things in the room, using the scale.

4 Chanelle wants to have a dressing table I m wide and 50 cm deep in her room. How could she fit it in?
   Choose the best place in the room to put it. Draw the dressing table on a copy of the plan at the correct scale. Add it to the key.

B | Photo of Chanelle's bedroom

Activities

5 Chanelle's family are thinking of selling their house. They invite an estate agent to advertise it. First, all the rooms have to be measured.

Measure each room in the house from the three floor plans. Notice the new scale. Draw an advertisement, like the one below, giving the size of each room.

LOUNGE	....
DINING ROOM	....
KITCHEN	....
BEDROOM 1	....
BEDROOM 2	....
BEDROOM 3	....
BEDROOM 4	....
BATHROOM	....

Homework

6 Draw a plan of your own bedroom. Include symbols, a key and a scale. Measure the room and the things in it, so that you draw it to the correct scale.

7 Measure the rooms in your own home. Draw a scale plan of each level in your home like the ones on this page.

Loft

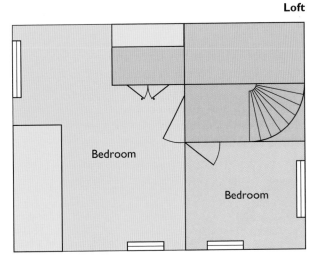

Upstairs

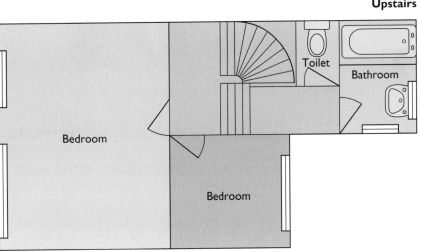

Downstairs

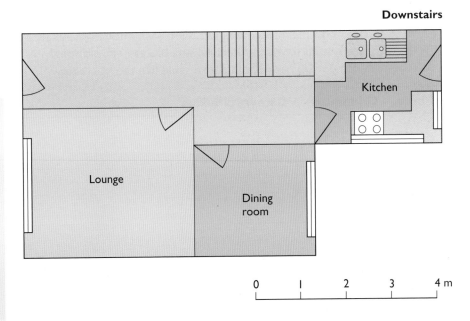

0   1   2   3   4 m

5

FRAMEWORK

1.3 **O**ut and about

Maps can help you find places. Most maps have an arrow that tells you the **direction** the map is facing. North is usually at the top of the map.

Some maps can be complicated, and an easier way to give directions is to use **grid squares**. Map E shows the area where Chanelle lives. The numbers and letters on the grid squares help you find places.

B

A

Activities

1 Look carefully at map E. Notice the direction and the scale on the map.

Find Chanelle's house. It is in square E5. Her school is in square B1–2.

2 Work out the best route for Chanelle to go to school. Which roads does she walk along? In which direction is she walking? How far must she walk?

Describe the route that Chanelle might walk to school. You could begin like this: Chanelle comes out of her house on Chestnut Avenue. She turns right and walks south-west for about 250 m. Then . . .

3 Look at the photos on this page. They were all taken somewhere on the map.

Find the place on the map where you think each photo was taken. Which square is it in? In which direction was the camera pointing? What evidence do you have? Complete a table like the one below.

C

Photo	Grid square	Camera direction	Evidence
A			
B			
C			
D			

Homework

4 Draw a sketch map of your journey to school. Describe the route that you take. (If you don't walk to school or your journey to school is long, choose a shorter journey that you often do.)

D

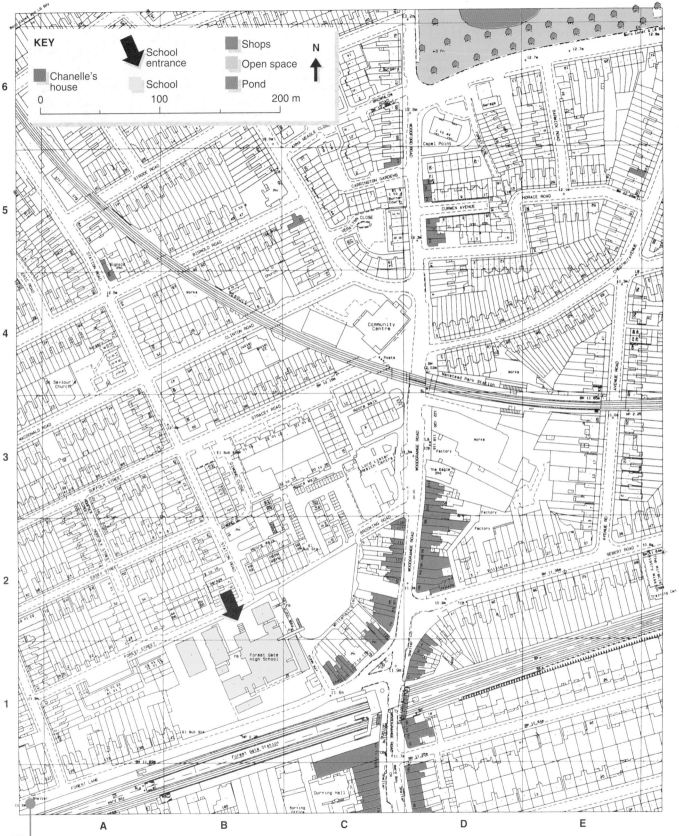

KEY

Chanelle's house

School entrance

School

Shops

Open space

Pond

N

0   100   200 m

E Forest Gate. Reproduced from the 1998 1:3,000 Ordnance Survey map of Forest Gate by permission of the Controller of HMSO © Crown Copyright

FRAMEWORK

1.4

The wider world

Maps can help you find out more about a place, even if you have never been there. An **atlas** is a book that has maps of many places around the world. Map A is an extract from an atlas map of south-east England, where Chanelle lives.

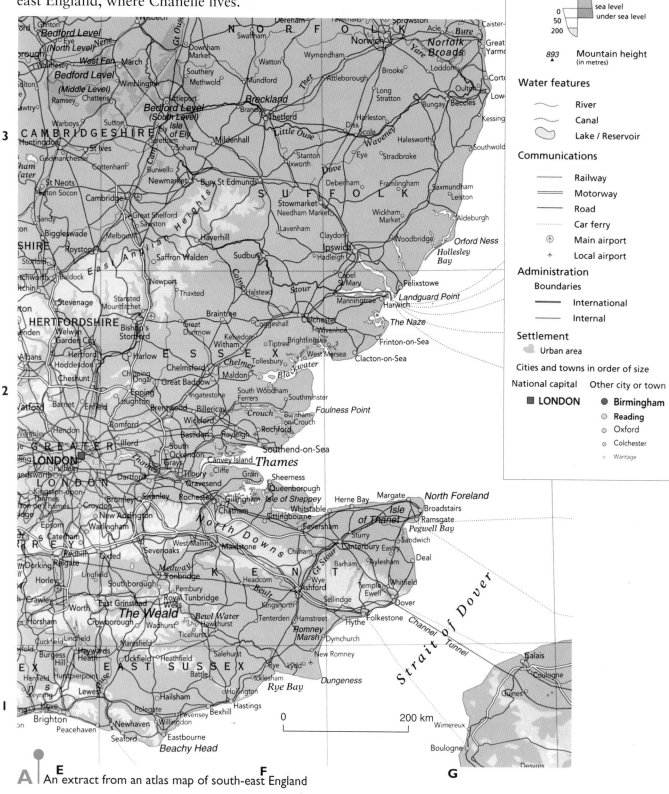

KEY

Relief and physical features

Relief metres
1000
500
200
100
sea level
0
50 under sea level
200

893 ▲ Mountain height (in metres)

Water features
~ River
~ Canal
Lake / Reservoir

Communications
Railway
Motorway
Road
Car ferry
⊕ Main airport
✈ Local airport

Administration
Boundaries
International
Internal

Settlement
Urban area

Cities and towns in order of size

National capital   Other city or town
■ **LONDON**   ● **Birmingham**
                    ● Reading
                    ○ Oxford
                    ○ Colchester
                    ○ Wantage

A An extract from an atlas map of south-east England

8

The contents page at the beginning of the atlas tells you what areas the maps on each page show. If you want to find a particular place, the quickest way is to use the index at the back of the atlas. This will tell you the page and the grid square in which to find the place. It will also tell you its **latitude** and **longitude**.

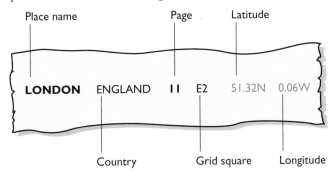

Place name · Page · Latitude

LONDON ENGLAND 11 E2 51.32N 0.06W

Country · Grid square · Longitude

Activities

1 Look at map A. Notice the key.

2 Find each of the following features on the map. Which grid squares are they in? Use the key to describe each feature.

London Thames North Downs Little Ouse Strait of Dover Norwich Channel Tunnel

Draw a table like the one below and complete it for all the features listed in the box.

Feature	Grid square	Description
London	E2	captial city

3 Find each of the features below in the index of your atlas. Which page are they on? What type of feature are they?

Everest Nile Los Angeles Sahara Pacific

Draw a table like the one above, giving the page number and the grid square for each feature.

Homework

4 Show why it is impossible to draw an accurate map of the world on a flat surface.

Draw the shapes of the continents onto an orange. Peel the orange carefully, trying to keep the peel in one piece. Lay the peel on a flat surface and try to make a map of the world. Draw the map that you make. Does it look like the map on this page?

Latitude and longitude

The most accurate way to show the whole Earth is on a **globe**, which is three-dimensional, like the world. Lines of latitude are imaginary lines going around the Earth from east to west. The line of latitude around the centre of the Earth is called the **Equator**. Latitude is measured in degrees north or south of the Equator. Lines of longitude are imaginary lines going from the North Pole to the South Pole. The line of longitude that goes through London is called the Greenwich Meridian. Longitude is measured in degrees east or west of the Greenwich Meridian. In this drawing of a globe you can only see half the Earth.

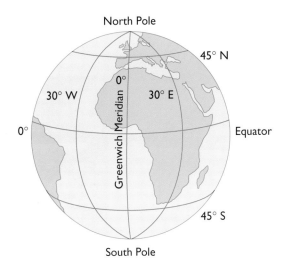

It is impossible to draw the earth accurately on a piece of paper, because the paper has a flat surface. Places will be either the wrong shape or the wrong size. This is the map of the world that you will see in *Earthworks*. Some places have been stretched and others have been squashed to make them fit.

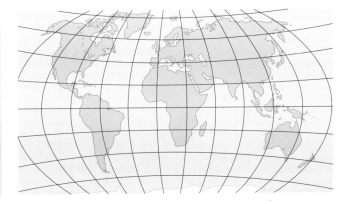

BUILDING BLOCKS

How well do you know your local area? In this Building Block you will study Chanelle's area. You could do similar activities in your own area.

Chanelle

1.5   **W**hat is the area like?

I live in an area called Forest Gate.
In case you don't know it, it's in east London, right at the top of the map you see on *EastEnders*. I've always lived here so I know the area pretty well. But if you asked me what it was like, I'd say it was kind of . . . you know . . . normal!
Recently my parents have started to talk about moving. It's getting serious. They've even called in an estate agent.
There are lots of things about this area I've never thought about before – some things I like, some I don't. It's all we talk about at home these days.

Forest Gate

A An aerial photo of Forest Gate

Chanelle's dad

Chanelle's brother and mum

Chanelle's gran

I suppose that living in Forest Gate is very handy for going to work in central London. We're only a five minute walk from the station and, on the train, I can be at work in half an hour. But the problem with living here is that we don't have a lot of space. I'd like to have a bigger garden and a garage to put the car in. Also most of the houses are about a hundred years old and they need repairs.

I'm worried about bringing the children up around here. There's nowhere for the little one to play. It's much too dangerous outside the house with cars parked all along the road and traffic whizzing by. There's no children's play space around here either. It's not so bad for Chanelle because there's a youth club that she can go to. Then there's the open space on Wanstead Flats, she loves kicking a ball around, and in the summer there's a fairground.

I came here nearly forty years ago. There have been so many changes since then. The biggest change is the amount of traffic that there is now. I'm glad I don't drive because I sometimes think it's quicker to walk! And those lorries and cars make so much dirt and noise. I'm lucky that I live so close to the shops. You can get most of what you need on the high street. But a few of my favourite shops have gone, like the old fishmonger's. Now that I've retired, I think it's time for me to go back to the West Indies.

Activities

1 Look at photo A. It is an aerial photo of Forest Gate where Chanelle lives. Compare the photo with map E on page 7. Can you find any of the features shown on the map in the photo?

2 Find each of the following features in the photo:

> a block of flats a railway line a busy high street
> an area of large detached houses a bridge
> an area of small terraced houses a school
> an area of open space a station

3 Read what members of Chanelle's family think about living in Forest Gate. Find evidence in photo A to support what they say.

4 Label an outline sketch of the photo, like the one here, to show the things that they mention. One is labelled for you.

Some of the things they mention are not in the photo. How would you investigate these?

5 Draw a table like the one below. List all the advantages (good points) and disadvantages (bad points) of living in Forest Gate.

Advantages (good points)	Disadvantages (bad points)

6 In a small group, talk about the area where you live. On a similar table, list all the advantages and disadvantages of living there.

BUILDING BLOCKS

Do you like your environment?

The area around you is your local **environment**. The same word – environment – is used to describe the whole world that surrounds us.

I asked my friends what they thought about living in the area. I got all sorts of answers – some positive, some negative.

safe · crowded · interesting · old · dirty · noisy · colourful · ugly

I remembered the work we are doing in geography at school. It's about **environmental quality**. I decided to try it out on my area.

Activities

1 Look at the environmental quality chart below. On a copy of the chart, complete the blank spaces with the words that Chanelle's friends used to describe the area.

	Very	Rather	Neither/nor	Rather	Very	
Negative words	–2	–1	0	+1	+2	**Positive words**
boring						
						beautiful
						clean
dull						
						new
						peaceful
dangerous						
						spacious
Totals						Total score

B

C

D

2 Look at photos B–E. How would you describe the environment in each one? Complete an environmental quality chart for each photo.

Give a score of between –2 and +2 for each pair of opposite words, for example if you think it is rather ugly score –1, if it is very colourful score +2.

Work out a total score for each photo by adding all the scores that you gave it. Which photo do you like best? Does everyone in your group agree?

 You may be able to record your scores on a spreadsheet, using a computer.

Homework

3 Do an environmental quality survey in your own local area.

E

. . . or could you improve it?

There are many ways to improve the environment.

G New houses. Older houses often need expensive repairs, such as a new roof or repainting. Many people prefer new houses.

F Pedestrianised high street. A shopping high street open to pedestrians and buses but not to cars. There is no traffic, so less dirt and noise. It is safer too.

H Car parks. Waste ground can be used for making a car park. This keeps traffic off the busy streets. It can also earn money to pay for other improvements.

I Children's play area. Waste ground can easily be changed into a play area. It should be easy for children and their parents to reach.

Activities

1 Look at the four suggestions for improving the environment. Which do you think is the most important? Why? What other improvements would you make?

2 Look again at map E on page 7. Can you find areas where you could make improvements? Are there any roads where you would change the traffic system? Are there any buildings you would demolish?

3 On a copy of the map, draw the improvements you would make.
   Use symbols on the map to show the improvements, for example, P could show a new car park. Draw a key for the map.

Homework

4 Suggest improvements that could be made in your local area. Draw a map to show the improvements you would make.

BUILDING BLOCKS

In this Building Block you will investigate one change that may happen in Chanelle's area.

1.6 How is the area changing?

Places are always changing. Many of the changes that happen in one area are the result of changes in the wider world.

Activities

1 Study the information on these two pages. It describes the new high-speed Channel Tunnel rail link, and its possible impact on Forest Gate. Compare the proposed route of the rail link with map E on page 7 and photo A on page 10.

2 Describe the possible impact of the new rail link on Forest Gate.
Suggest:
a) Why the rail link may tunnel under Forest Gate
b) What its impact might be at the following points along the route through south-east England.

> The North Downs   a village like Cobham
> a town with a new station, like Ashford

3 Work in a small group.
   Role play a conversation Chanelle's family might have about the new rail link. Each person should play one member of the family. Look back to page 11 to remind yourself who they are and what they think about Forest Gate. Think about how they might feel about the changes. As a family, decide whether the changes would make you more likely or less likely to want to stay in the area.
   You could introduce extra characters into the conversation, such as an uncle who is out of work, a local shopkeeper, or a friend who works in the fashion business.

Like many other areas in cities, Forest Gate developed about 100 years ago because of the new railway lines that were being built. People were able to travel into London every day by train. Many came to live in Forest Gate. Now a new rail route could bring more change to the area.

> The big change in our area is the plan for a new Channel Tunnel Rail Link from St Pancras Station in central London to the Channel Tunnel in Kent. It could go right under Forest Gate! There may even be a big new international station near here – at Stratford. That's another reason my parents say that they want to move. But I don't think it's all that bad. And I'll be able to hop on a train to Paris!

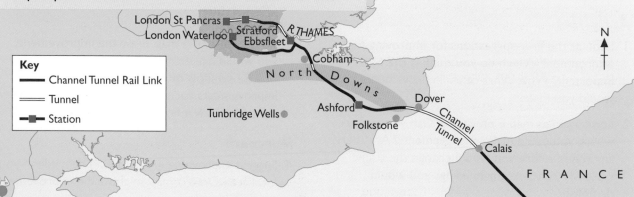

Key
— Channel Tunnel Rail Link
= Tunnel
■– Station

London St Pancras
London Waterloo
Stratford
Ebbsfleet
R. THAMES
Cobham
North Downs
Tunbridge Wells
Ashford
Dover
Folkstone
Channel Tunnel
Calais
FRANCE

0   50 km

N

A The proposed Channel Tunnel Rail Link through south-east England

... and who will the changes affect?

EAST LONDON ADVERTISER   4 December 1997

NEW RAIL ROUTE ROW

Key
- ▪ ▪ ▪ Route of Channel Tunnel Rail Link
- ⎯⎯ Other rail routes

0   500 m

Stratford International Station

Stratford Station

FOREST GATE

Woodgrange Road

Osborne Road

Romford Road

N

Local investigation

What is the impact of one change in your local area?

Follow these guidelines to carry out a geographical investigation in your local area.

1 Identify a question or issue that you want to investigate, for example the impact of a new road, a new flood barrier, a new cinema.

2 Think about what information you will need to investigate the issue and where you can find it. Consider maps, photos, aerial photos, data, people's opinions, etc. You could collect your own information, for example, do an environmental quality survey, take photos, carry out interviews, or use libraries, newspapers, the Internet to find it.

   Collect, record and present the information in the form of maps, photos, diagrams, data tables, etc., possibly with the help of a computer.

3 Think about your findings and write your conclusion. Consider the following:
   - Has the area improved or got worse?
   - How has this happened?
   - Is everybody affected in the same way?
   - Which groups of people are affected, and how?

The Government has at last confirmed the proposed route of the new high-speed rail link from London to the Channel Tunnel. The decision on the route, which includes a major new station at Stratford in east London, could bring more money and jobs to the area. The railway will travel 30 m below Forest Gate on its way from central London to the Channel Tunnel in Kent.

Reaction to the news among the local public was mixed. Shop-owners on Woodgrange Road in Forest Gate are worried. One predicted, 'There might be an increase in trade which would be good news, but there will be so much more traffic that we won't be able to move – not above ground anyway!' A resident on Osborne Road said, 'We don't know how it will affect our homes. Trains will be going under our living rooms at 100 miles (160 km) per hour. House prices will fall because no one will want to buy around here.' Worst affected could be the people who live just west of Woodgrange Road. A ventilation shaft to be constructed in this area will lead to extra dirt, noise and vibration. Some properties will have to be demolished to make space for it.

But a spokesman for the local council said, 'We welcome the news. It will bring a much needed boost to the area. The number of people in this area without work is one of the highest in London. This will create thousands of new jobs, both during the construction of the tunnel, and when the new station opens. A lot of new business will be attracted to Stratford and the area around it.'

BUILDING BLOCKS

In this Building Block you will compare two local areas and decide where you would prefer to live.

N. America

St Lucia

S. America

1.7 **Would you stay?**

Gran is trying to persuade my parents that they ought to go back to the West Indies with her. She comes from the island of St Lucia. I can't believe it! I mean, my mum was only about two when she left, and the rest of us have never been there. I learnt about it in primary school once – warm sun, tropical rainforest, sandy beaches, all that sort of stuff – but to live there . . . it's mind-blowing! My mum thinks it might be a good idea, because they're more strict in school. Huh, that's not a good enough reason! And dad says he doesn't mind if he gets a bigger garden! Apparently there's jobs for people with his computer skills. I haven't decided what I think yet, but I've got lots of questions.

Activities

1 Read the list of questions that Chanelle would like to ask about St Lucia. Which questions do you think are most important? Rank the questions in order of importance. Think of other questions you would like to ask. Include them in your list.

2 Find a map of St Lucia in your atlas. What does the map tell you about it?

3 Study the data below, and the maps and photos on the opposite page. Use them to help you answer the questions for yourself.

What is the weather like?

Where is it?   How do you get around?

What jobs do people do?   What people live there?

What is the environment like?

What can you do in your spare time?

ST LUCIA DATAFILE

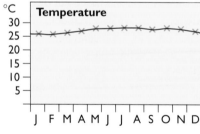

Temperature

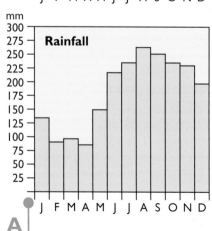

Rainfall

Land

Key
- Town
- Forest
- Bananas
- Other farms

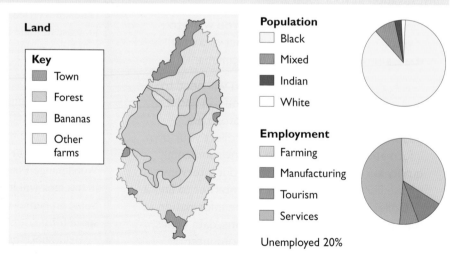

Population
- Black
- Mixed
- Indian
- White

Employment
- Farming
- Manufacturing
- Tourism
- Services

Unemployed 20%

Assignment

Either: Compare Forest Gate, Chanelle's local area, with St Lucia. Decide where she might prefer to live. Give some reasons.

Or: Compare your own local area with St Lucia. Decide where you would prefer to live. Give your reasons.

A

... or would you go?

B | A view of Castries harbour

C | Reduit Bay, a tourist beach

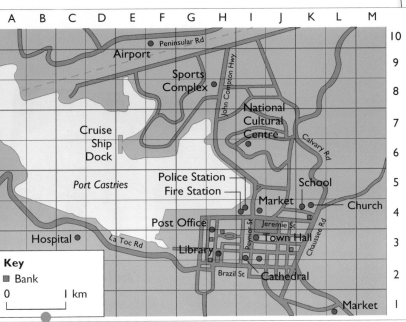

D | Castries

Map labels for D:

A B C D E F G H I J K L M

10 9 8 7 6 5 4 3 2 1

Peninsular Rd
Airport
Sports Complex
John Compton Hwy
National Cultural Centre
Calvary Rd
Cruise Ship Dock
Port Castries
Police Station
Fire Station
School
Market
Church
Post Office
Jeremie St
Peynier St
Chaussee Rd
Hospital
La Toc Rd
Library
Town Hall
Brazil St
Cathedral
Market

Key
■ Bank
0   1 km

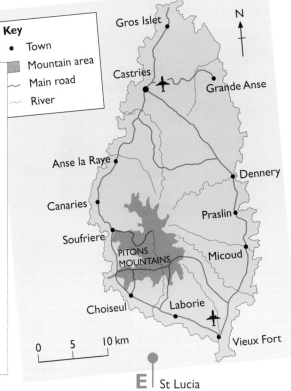

E | St Lucia

Key
• Town
Mountain area
Main road
River

N

Gros Islet
Castries
Grande Anse
Anse la Raye
Dennery
Canaries
Praslin
Soufriere
Micoud
PITONS MOUNTAINS
Choiseul
Laborie
Vieux Fort

0   5   10 km

F | A residential area of Castries

G | The market in Castries

DIGGING DEEPER

1.8 One country – contrasting regions

It's not surprising if your local area is very different to an area in another country, but just how different are areas within your own country?

The UK is divided into **regions**, which are shown on map D. Each region covers an area with similar geographical characteristics, such as landscape, climate and the types of work people do. People living in a particular region may share the same history and culture or, in some cases, may even speak their own language. The region that you live in may also affect your **quality of life**.

Scotland

B

South-east England

A Kent

D UK regions

C Edinburgh

E People in Glasgow

F

G Industry on the River Thames

Activities

1 Look at map D of the UK regions. The cartoon drawings show some images that people often have about two regions – Scotland and the South-east.

2 For each region compare the cartoons with the photos. How do they differ? Which image do you think gives the most accurate picture of each region? Why?

   What other sources of information would you use to find out more about a region?

3 Choose another region in the UK, apart from the one that you live in. Draw cartoons or sketches to show your image of that region.

   Then investigate the region with the help of an atlas and other sources of information. Find out as much as you can about landscape, climate, employment and other characteristics of the region. Has your image of the region changed at all? In what way?

Scotland

Temperature and rainfall – Oban

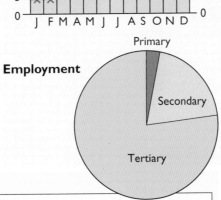

Employment

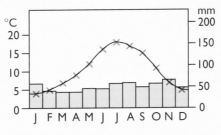

Area and population

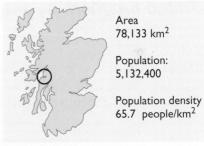

Area
78,133 km^2

Population:
5,132,400

Population density
65.7 people/km^2

Facts and figures

- Scotland is the least crowded region in the UK. There were 2 per cent fewer people in 1994 than in 1971.
- Scotland is the wettest region in the UK.
- School pupils in Scotland achieve better exam grades than pupils in any other UK region.
- Deaths from cancer are higher in Scotland than in any other UK region.
- More people in Scotland take a foreign holiday than people in any other UK region.

Source: *Regional Trends 1996*, Office for National Statistics

South-east England

Facts and figures

- The south-east is the most crowded region in the UK. There are over 1,000 people per km^2 in London.
- The south-east is the warmest region in the UK.
- Men in the south-east are the highest paid in the UK. They also work the shortest number of hours.
- More money is spent on schools in the south-east, per pupil, than in any other UK region.
- Households in the south-east are more likely to have a CD player and a computer than in any other UK region.

Employment

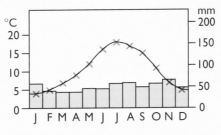

Temperature and rainfall – London

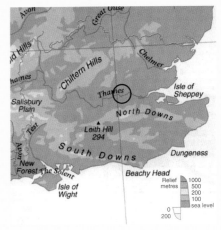

Area and population

Area
27,224 km^2

Population:
17,870,200

Population density
656 people/km^2

Activities

Work with a partner, or in a small group.

1 Discuss what you think is meant by the term 'quality of life'. What things have most effect on the quality of life in a region? You can include any of the ideas on this page and page 20.

2 Compare Scotland and south-east England. From the evidence on these pages which region has the best quality of life, do you think? Give your reasons. Can you suggest any problems in using this evidence to compare the quality of life in two regions?

3 Produce a leaflet for one region in the UK, to persuade people to move there.

DIGGING DEEPER

United Kingdom or divided nation?

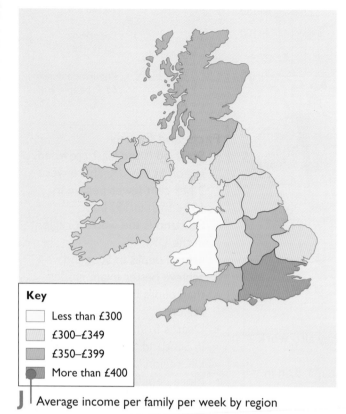

Key

☐	Less than £300
☐	£300–£349
☐	£350–£399
■	More than £400

J Average income per family per week by region

In the 1980s, it used to be said that the UK was divided into two parts: the rich 'south' and the poor 'north'. The 'south' included south-east and south-west England, East Anglia and also the West and East Midlands. It was the part of the UK with a better quality of life, lower unemployment and where most of the new industries were growing. By contrast, the rest of the country, which was the 'north', had a worse quality of life, higher unemployment and more traditional industries which, in the 1980s, were quickly disappearing. Could the same be said today?

Map J shows the average weekly income for families in each region in 1995. The darker the colour on the map the higher the income. Income is one way to compare quality of life.

Activities

1 Look at map J. It shows the average income per family in each region. Do you notice any difference between 'north' and 'south'?
2 Look at the data in table K. It shows four other indicators of the quality of life in each region. Draw maps to show the regional differences for each of the indicators in the table. For each map:
   a) Choose a colour.
   b) Find out the range of the data, for example, average house price varies from £42,900 to £80,000 between regions.
   c) Divide the range into three or four bands, for example, house prices: less than £50,000, £50,000–£59,999, £60,000–£69,999, £70,000 and over.
   d) Colour each map according to the data in the table. Use a different shade for each band. The higher it is, the darker it should be. Complete a key for each map.

Region	Average house price (£ 000)	Unemploy-ment (%)	Families with one or more cars (%)	Crimes recorded (per 100,000 people)
North	46.1	10.6	59	12,678
Yorkshire	52.6	8.8	67	12,860
East Midlands	53.3	7.7	69	10,851
East Anglia	59.0	6.2	76	7,508
South-east	80.0	7.9	71	9,597
South-west	64.0	7.0	75	9,046
West Midlands	60.5	8.4	69	10,134
North-west	55.5	8.8	64	10,560
Wales	52.5	8.5	67	8,988
Scotland	52.7	8.2	62	10,269
Northern Ireland	42.9	11.4	65	4,134

Source: *Regional Trends 1996*, Office for National Statistics

K Regional differences in quality of life

Assignment

Write a report entitled 'Does it matter where you live in the UK?' Use the titles of your maps as the headings for your paragraphs. Describe the patterns that you can see in the maps. As a conclusion, consider which regions of the UK have the best quality of life, and which have the worst. Give your reasons.

Near Southwold, on the east coast of England

These **cliffs** look as if they have always been there, but the
coastline of Britain is slowly changing.
- Would you like to live here? Why?
- Where do you think the coastline was thousands of years ago?
- Where will it be thousands of years from now?
- What is causing the landscape to change?

GROUNDWORK

2.1 Is your school breaking up?

Nothing stays the same for ever. Everything – even the landscape – changes. Most of these changes are so slow that you might not notice them taking place, but over thousands of years even the most solid rock can change. All the forces of nature – sun, water, ice and wind – bring about changes to the landscape, breaking up the surface and wearing it away.

All the **processes** that change the natural landscape also work on buildings. They are probably happening in your school. Sun, rain, frost, wind, and even plants can attack buildings, causing them to break up or crumble. This process is called **weathering**.

B Cement crumbles. Rain, which behaves like a very weak acid, slowly eats away at the cement. Buildings made from limestone are attacked in the same way.

A Paint peels from walls, doors and window frames. Changes of temperature – especially if the weather is very hot or very cold – cause paint to expand and to shrink. This makes it crack and peel from the surface beneath.

Activities

1 Look at photos A, B and C. Each one shows a different type of weathering on a school building. Match each photo with a type of weathering:
   - **Physical weathering** – caused by changes in temperature
   - **Chemical weathering** – caused by the action of water
   - **Biological weathering** – caused by the action of plants or animals.

2 Examine your own school, or your local area. How many examples of weathering can you find?
   a) Draw sketches to show any examples that you find.
   b) Mark the places where you find them onto a map.
   c) Suggest the cause of weathering in each case. What could be done to slow down the processes of weathering in your school or your area?

C Plants such as mosses and lichens grow on roofs and walls. They send their roots into the tiles or bricks, which makes them slowly crumble. As the surface breaks up, it makes way for larger plants to grow.

Another process that changes the landscape is **erosion**. In the natural landscape this is mainly due to rivers, the sea, ice or wind wearing away rock.

People are also an important cause of erosion. The more people that move over a surface the quicker it is likely to be eroded. Think of a football pitch. At the end of the football season the grass is usually most worn away around the two goalmouths. This is where most of the action happens in a game of football.

D | Erosion caused by pupils

E | Pupils in the playground

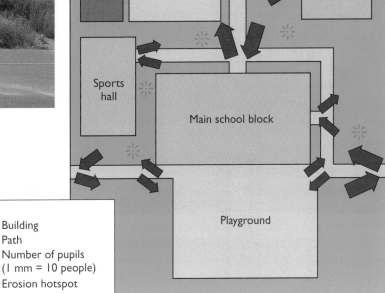

Key

■ Building
■ Path
◤ Number of pupils (1 mm = 10 people)
✳ Erosion hotspot

F | Movement of pupils around a school

Activities

1 Look at the photos and the map above. Map F shows the movement of pupils around a school during one morning break. It also shows the places with most erosion – the erosion hotspots.

2 With your class, investigate movement and erosion in your own school.

Work in pairs. Each pair should stand at a different location in the school grounds at break or lunchtime.

Count the number of pupils that pass by in one direction. Your partner can count the number of pupils moving in the other direction. Look at the area where you are standing. Can you see any erosion that might be caused by pupils, such as grass worn away, or hedges damaged?

Bring together all the information gathered by the members of your class.

Complete a map of your school to show the movement of pupils, like the one above. The width of the arrows shows the number of pupils travelling in each direction. Mark the places where you found erosion.

3 Compare the movement of pupils around the school with the areas where there is erosion. What do you notice? How do you explain this?

Homework

4 What examples of natural erosion can you find in your local area?

FRAMEWORK

2.2

Shaping the landscape

Weathering and erosion work together to shape the natural landscape. Weathering breaks up the Earth's surface. Cycles of cold and hot freeze and thaw the rock causing it to crack. Rainfall and living plants and animals cause rock to crumble. Erosion then wears away the loose rock. Water, ice and wind all erode the landscape. Over thousands of years they slowly change its shape. Each type of erosion produces its own particular **landforms**.

B The sea meets the land at the coast. Large **waves** hit the base of cliffs with tremendous force. This compresses air into cracks in the rock so that the rock shatters. The large pieces are broken up and become smoothed and rounded as they hit each other. The sea slowly shapes the coastline, forming bays and headlands.

A Rivers pick up small pieces of rock and carry them along. As these move they bump into each other and are rounded into pebbles. They grind the rock at the bottom and sides of the river, slowly wearing it away. Rivers can erode the landscape to form V-shaped valleys.

C Ice often collects high in mountains. It may form glaciers, which are slow-moving rivers of ice. They carry with them huge amounts of rock, ranging from bits of sand to enormous boulders. Sharp points on these scrape the surface beneath as the glacier flows, like a giant chisel. When glaciers melt, they leave deep U-shaped valleys.

D Wind, blowing across dry areas like deserts, picks up tiny particles of dust and sand. Any large rock that falls in the wind's path is blasted by the wind. The sand and dust sometimes erode rocks into unusual shapes which are characteristic of deserts.

Activities

1   Study photos A–D, and the descriptions of different types of erosion. Which of the tools in diagram E best describes the action of each type of erosion? What landform does each type of erosion produce?

2   Draw a table, like the one below. List the types of erosion shown in the photos in the first column. Complete the next three columns with words and drawings. One example has been started for you.

    Describe how each type of erosion works. Try to use your own words.

Chisel

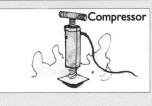
Grinder

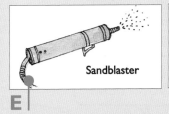
Sandblaster   Compressor

E

Type of erosion	Action is like?	Rock sample	Landform	Description
River	grinder	small pebble	V-shaped valley	

3   Look at photos F and G. They show two cliffs – one made of hard rock, the other of soft rock. How can you tell which is which?

    Draw a sketch of photo F, like the one below. Choose the correct labels from the box below to add to the sketch.

    Draw a sketch of photo G. Add the correct labels.

cliff made of hard rock	cliff made of soft rock
waves slowly erode cliff	waves quickly erode cliff

F   Chalk cliffs at Beachy Head, Sussex

Homework

4   Find out how difficult it is to erode different types of material. Choose materials that you can find at home or at school. Here are some you could try: chalk, wood, plastic, soap, steel, clay.

    Rub each one with sandpaper. How easily do they erode?

    List them in order of how difficult they are to erode, with the hardest at the top.

G   Clay cliffs on East Yorkshire coast

2.3 Changing coastline

The sea is constantly changing the shape of the land. When Julius Caesar, commander of the Roman army, landed in Britain over 2,000 years ago, the coastline on which he landed was not the same as it is today. Places which were on the coast then are no longer there. Some have disappeared altogether, washed away as the sea has eroded the land. Others are now found far inland, where the sea has built up new land.

FUNNY...I'M SURE I LEFT MY SHIP SOMEWHERE ROUND HERE!

Where large waves crash against the coast, the sea changes the coastline by erosion. Soft rock is worn away to form **bays** while harder rock remains, jutting into the sea, as **headlands**. The sea transports the material it has eroded and deposits it in places where the water is calm. These three processes – erosion, **transportation** and **deposition** – are happening all around the coast of Britain.

A | South-west Wales

Strumble Head   Fishguard Bay
St David's Head
St Bride's Bay
St Anne's Head
Carmarthen Bay

0   10 km   St Govan's Head

Key
- hard sandstone
- slate
- limestone
- mixed
- basalt
- granite

Activities

1. Look at map A of south-west Wales. It shows the different types of rock found in the area. This is a **geology** map.

   What do you notice about the shape of the coastline? What features have been formed? Where do you think the rock is hardest?

2. Look at photos B, C and D on the next page. Compare them with diagram E.

   Identify the landforms shown in the photos. In which order would these landforms have been made? In the correct order, draw a simple sketch of each photo. Label the landforms.

3. With the help of diagram E, explain how each of the landforms in the photos might have been formed. Write a sentence about each one. Choose words from the box below to use in your sentences.

   > shatter hollow fall waves collapse
   > attack pillar widen compress weathered
   > force headland

4. Look at photo F. It shows a beach near Flamborough Head.

   Explain why the beach might be here. Where did the material come from?

B The coast near Flamborough Head, Yorkshire

C

D

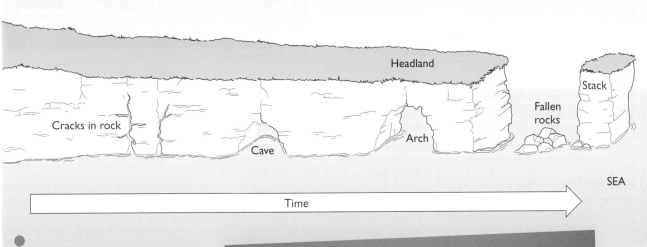

Headland

Stack

Cracks in rock

Fallen rocks

Cave

Arch

SEA

Time

E Stages in the erosion of a headland

The sea deposits material around the coast to form **beaches**. The material can be any size from the finest sand to large stones. All of it has been eroded from other parts of the coastline. Beaches are often found in bays where the waves are smaller, so the sea is more likely to deposit.

F A beach near Flamborough Head

FRAMEWORK

2.4 Cliff collapse!

Living near the coast is meant to be good for your health. It can also be very dangerous! Occasionally, the dangers of being near the sea are headline news.

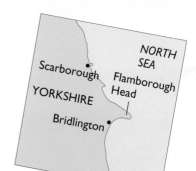

YORKSHIRE DAILY NEWS

Saturday 5th June, 1993

HOTEL FALLS INTO THE SEA

A four-star hotel was, last night, falling into the sea after a 1 km section of the cliff top at Scarborough collapsed into the sea. Holbeck Hall, which has stood overlooking the North Sea for more than a hundred years, has been gradually falling apart since the collapse began in the early hours of yesterday morning.

Eighty guests, who had each paid £100 a night to stay at the hotel, had to be woken early to evacuate the hotel. One guest commented, 'I hardly had time to pack my bags. I looked out of the window and I could see that half of the lawn had vanished. I didn't need to be persuaded to leave!' Guests were asked to settle their bills as they left, but they were not charged for breakfast. By lunchtime, half of the hotel, including its new restaurant, had disappeared over the edge of the cliff.

The destruction of the hotel was particularly surprising as it lay 100 m from the cliff edge. Michael Clements, Scarborough's director of technical services, explained: 'The fall was due to a landslip in the cliffs. They're made of clay, and after a few dry summers they begin to develop cracks. It only takes a wet winter, like the one we've just had, to let water into the cracks and then they begin to slip.' Other home owners near Holbeck Hall have expressed their concern. They want to know how safe their own properties will be. Engineers are due to begin tests on the cliff today to see if the ground is still moving. They will then have to decide on the best way to stabilise the cliffs to prevent them slipping again.

This is not the first time a building on the east coast of Yorkshire has fallen into the sea. Along the coast, south of Flamborough Head, whole villages have been lost as a result of coastal erosion. Up to 2 m of land is lost each year in this way. A geologist from Hull University said, 'It is unusual for such a large chunk of land to disappear at one time, but we have to expect events like this to happen every now and again. We can build sea walls to try to protect the cliffs, but whatever we do the sea will continue to erode the coast. All we can do is delay it for a bit longer.'

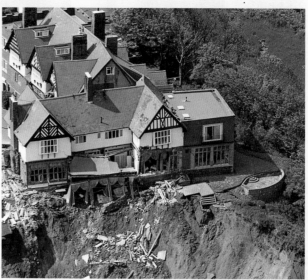

The final moments as the hotel falls into the sea

Before and after the collapse

Protecting the coast

For centuries people have tried to protect the coast from the power of the sea. Seaside towns are often protected by strong **sea walls**, but even these may be no match for the waves on a stormy sea. A better understanding of how the sea works and of the geology of the coastline may help to protect the coast.

A The sea wall at Scarborough

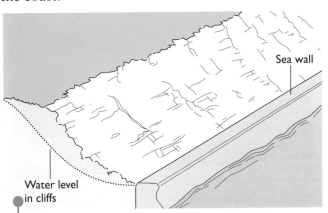

B Cliffs can be protected by building a sea wall in front of them. The wall prevents the waves from eroding the base of the cliff. It deflects the power of the waves away from the coast and back to the sea.

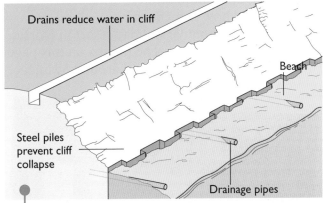

C Cliffs can be drained to reduce the amount of water in them. Drains near the cliff top take water away before it can seep into the cliff. Steel barriers hammered into the rock near the base of the cliff collect the remaining water, which drains out through pipes.

Activities

1 Study the newspaper article on the opposite page. Which of the statements below could be used to explain why the hotel fell into the sea?
   a) There was a severe storm.
   b) Water had seeped into the cliff.
   c) The hotel was right at the edge of the cliff.
   d) The cliff had become unstable.
   e) The cliff was made of hard limestone.
   f) The cliff was made of soft clay.
   g) The cliff had become stable.
   h) There was a landslip in the cliff.
   i) There is no sea wall at Scarborough.

2 Look at the two methods of protecting the coast shown in diagrams B and C. Which might be the best method to prevent further cliff collapses in the area near Holbeck Hall Hotel? Explain why this method might work.

3 Work in a small group.
   Imagine that you are a TV news crew, sent to Scarborough after the hotel fell into the sea. You have been asked to find out:
   • What happened
   • Why it happened
   • Whether it could happen again
   • How it could be prevented from happening again.

Interview people mentioned in the newspaper article to find out the answers to your questions. Take turns to play the roles of the interviewer and the people being interviewed.

In this Building Block you will use a map and photos to identify coastal features, and explain how they were formed.

2.5 What can you see beside the sea?

Holidays are a good time to do geography. Many people go to the seaside for their holiday, either in this country or abroad. If you go to the coast, you may be able to see some of the coastal landforms that you have met in this unit, and you could ask a few geographical questions – what is it?, why is it there?, and how is it changing?

Swanage is a popular holiday resort in Dorset, in the south of England. The photos on this page were taken on the coast in and around Swanage.

A

B

C

D

Activities

1 Look at photos A–D. What landforms can you identify in them?

2 Look at map E on the opposite page. It shows the coast near Swanage. Follow the south-west coast path from The Foreland (in grid square 0582) to Durlston Head (in grid square 0377).
   Match each photo with one of these grid squares on the map: 0377, 0378, 0582, 0379. Give the correct name for each place.

3 Describe the walk along the coast path from The Foreland to Durlston Head. Break the walk into sections. For each section:
   a) Measure the distance, using the scale.
   b) Say in which direction you are walking.
   c) Mention any interesting features you pass on the way.

BUILDING BLOCKS

Why is it there?

The geology, or rocks, around Swanage can help to explain the landforms that are found in the area. Like most of southern and eastern England, it is made of **sedimentary rocks** that were formed millions of years ago by material (or sediment) deposited on the sea bed. Each layer of rock represents a different period of geological history. Chalk, limestone, sandstone and clay are all types of sedimentary rock. Since they were laid down, the rocks have been pushed up and folded by powerful forces deep within the Earth.

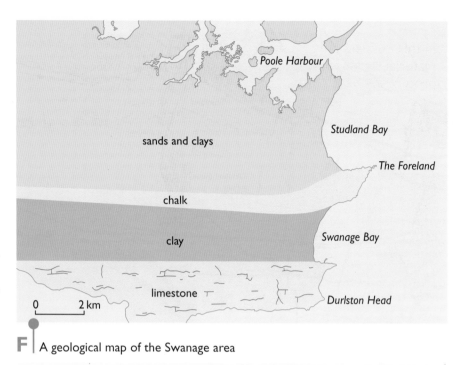

F A geological map of the Swanage area

G The Foreland, near Swanage

Activities

I Look at map F. It is a geological map of the Swanage area. What type of rock is found around:
   a) The Foreland
   b) Swanage Bay
   c) Durlston Head
   d) Studland Bay?
   Which of these rocks do you think are hard, and which soft? Give your reasons.
      Using the photos on page 30, can you describe any features of these rocks?

2 Look at drawing G, which shows The Foreland as it is today.
      Draw a sketch to show what it may have looked like thousands of years ago, before Old Harry was formed. Explain any changes that have taken place.
      Draw another sketch to show what it may look like thousands of years from now, after Old Harry has been eroded. Explain why this may happen.

Assignment

Produce an information leaflet for people coming to Swanage. It could include:
- Directions for people travelling to Swanage by car
- Places where they could stay
- A description of a walk along the coast
- Other activities they could do
- An explanation of how some of the coastal landforms were formed.

Use map E on the previous page to help you.

 You can use a desktop publishing package on a computer to help you to produce the leaflet.

In this Building Block you will find out how the sea moves material on a beach. You will use your findings to suggest how to protect the beach.

2.6 Is the sand shifting?

We have been on a field trip to the south coast with our school. One of our tasks was to investigate whether the sand on the beach moves. Our teacher explained that many people in the area depend on tourism for their jobs. They are worried that beaches are losing their sand, and that if the beaches disappeared then tourists would stop coming.

A Pupils were given some equipment and asked to think of how they could use it to find out if the sand really is moving.

Activity

Work in a small group.

Study the information on this page. Think about how you could find out if the sand on the beach is moving and, if it is, where it is going. You can use any of the equipment that the teacher has provided.

Describe how you would investigate this question and what equipment you would use. *Clue:* the pupils did two different experiments and used all the equipment.

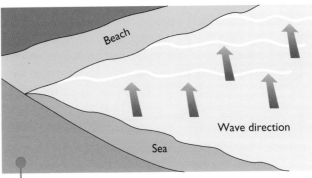

B Wind moving over the surface of the sea makes waves. As the waves hit the coastline they break, and roll up the beach. This is the **swash**.

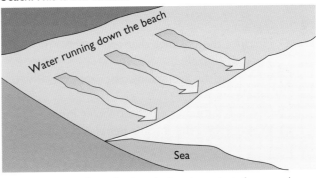

As the waves roll up the beach they lose their force and gravity drags the water back down the beach. This is the **backwash**.

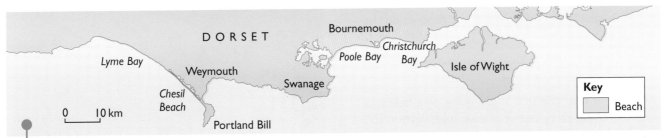

C Part of the south coast of England

BUILDING BLOCKS

How does the beach move?

We did two investigations on the beach.
First, we painted a pile of pebbles with bright red paint so that they would show up clearly on the beach. When the paint was dry and the tide was out we placed them in a line down the beach. We marked the line with one of the poles at the top of the beach. At the end of the day we came back to the beach to try to find the pebbles. None of them were in their original place. Many of them had disappeared, but we did find some. We measured the distance they had moved along the beach from the original line.

How did the pebbles move?
We did the second investigation to find out.
We put a ball in the sea at the edge of the beach, and marked its position with a pole which we pushed into the sand. We followed the movement of the ball as it was carried up and down the beach by the swash and backwash of the waves. Each time it changed direction we marked the position with another pole. After we had done that about 20 times we looked at the pattern that the poles made.

Activities

1 Read how the pupils investigated the movement of sand on the beach. Was their investigation similar to your ideas?

Look at diagrams D and E which show the results of their investigations.

2 In diagram D:
   a) Measure the distance that each pebble moved along the beach.
   b) Work out the average distance that the pebbles moved.
   c) In which direction did the pebbles move?
   d) Where might the missing pebbles have gone?

3 In diagram E:
   a) Describe the pattern made by the ball as it moved in the sea.
   b) In which direction did the ball move?
   c) How does the movement of the ball help to explain the movement of the pebbles on the beach?

Local investigation

If you live near the sea, or are going on a field trip to the coast, carry out your own investigation to find out how material moves on the beach.

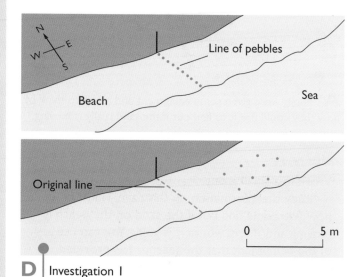

D | Investigation 1

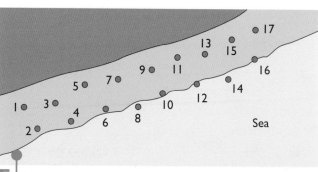

E | Investigation 2

... and can it be stopped?

The pupils' investigations showed that sand does move along the beach. This process is called **longshore drift**. It happens when waves move towards the coast at an angle, blown in that direction by the wind. The swash carries material up the beach at the same angle. The backwash carries material straight back down the beach as it runs to the sea. So, as the waves go in and out, material moves along the beach in a zig-zag pattern, rather like the ball in Investigation 2.

Longshore drift moves sand, pebbles and other material along the coastline. The material that is lost from the beach is normally replaced by material that has been eroded from another part of the coast. But, if the natural supply of material was stopped, then the beach would eventually disappear.

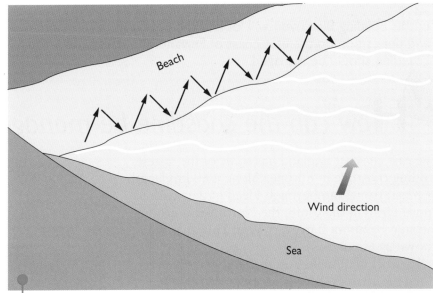

F The process of longshore drift

G The beach at Poole on the south coast. Wooden **groynes** slow down the movement of sand along the coast.

Activities

1 Look at diagram F. Compare it with diagram B on page 33. Use the two diagrams to describe the process of longshore drift in your own words.

2 Look at photo G. Draw a sketch of the beach. Add the following labels:

> waves groyne
> beach builds up on one side of the groyne
> beach is narrow on other side of groyne

Explain how your sketch shows longshore drift at work. Draw an arrow on the sketch to show the direction of longshore drift along the coast.

3 Explain how groynes can be used to slow down longshore drift. What is the advantage of building groynes? Can you think of any disadvantages?

Assignment

Write a report for a seaside town on the south coast of England, recommending how it could protect its beach.

On a map of the south coast, draw an arrow to show the direction of longshore drift. (The wind is mainly from the south-west.)

Explain how groynes might be able to help. Suggest what effect this could have:
a) On the town itself
b) On places further east along the coast.

In this Building Block you will look at the processes of erosion and deposition on the east coast of England, and decide how the coastline should be managed.

— Mappleton

2.7 How can the coastline be managed?

The east coast of England has some of the fastest eroding coastline in Europe. Along a 60 km length of coast, from Flamborough Head in the north to Spurn Head in the south, the North Sea is eroding the land by about 2 m every year. This area is known as Holderness.

The rock that makes up the land and the cliffs along the coast is soft boulder clay, left by the glaciers at the end of the last Ice Age, 10,000 years ago. It is easily worn away by the heavy waves that pound it.

Over the last 2,000 years, many villages along this coast have disappeared into the North Sea as the coastline has moved back. The process is still going on. Recently, the village of Mappleton looked likely to become the latest victim. But pressure from its residents, afraid of losing their homes, eventually led to new groynes being built to protect the beach and save the village.

A | Eroding coastline near Mappleton

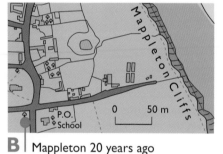

B | Mappleton 20 years ago

C | Mappleton today

D | The changing Yorkshire coastline

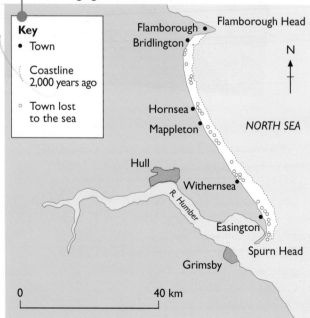

Key
● Town

⸰⸰⸰ Coastline 2,000 years ago

○ Town lost to the sea

0 _____ 40 km

Activities

1 Look at maps B and C. How far has the coastline at Mappleton moved back over the last 20 years? How many buildings have been lost?
   On a copy of the map of Mappleton today, draw a line to show where the coastline might be in 20 years' time if no sea defences had been built.

2 Imagine that you live in Mappleton. How would you feel about living there? Do you think that the new sea defences are a good idea? Why?

3 Look at map D. It shows how the coastline has changed since Roman times. How far has the coastline moved back? How many towns have been lost? Which towns and villages appear to be in greatest danger now? Which parts of the coast have not been eroded? Can you suggest why?

Winds blowing from the north-east across the North Sea bring waves that hit the coast at an angle. This causes longshore drift. Much of the material that is eroded from the cliffs is mud which gets washed out to sea. The sea offshore is often stained brown by the mud that it carries. The remaining sand is transported south along the coast until it is deposited. Much of it ends up at Spurn Head, a **spit** which lies across the mouth of the River Humber. A spit is really an extended beach which continues the coastline across a bay or river mouth. The area behind the spit is sheltered and begins to collect mud, forming new marshland where plants can grow. However, on the seaward side, heavy storms can easily break through the spit, washing away the sand from which it is built.

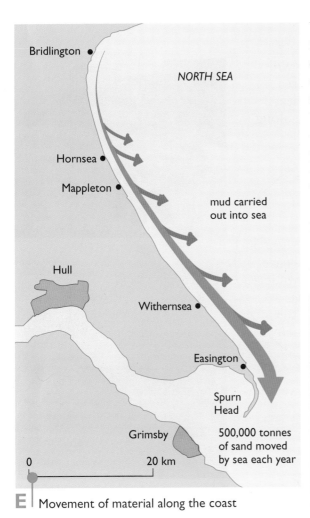

E | Movement of material along the coast

NORTH SEA

Bridlington

Hornsea

Mappleton

mud carried out into sea

Hull

Withernsea

Easington

Spurn Head

Grimsby

500,000 tonnes of sand moved by sea each year

0   20 km

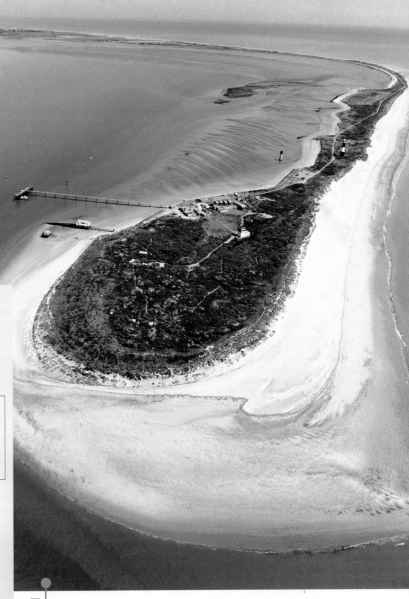

F | Spurn Head

Activities

1 Look at the aerial photo of Spurn Head.
   Draw a simple sketch map of the area in the photo. Add the labels in the box below to the correct places on your map:

> material transported along coast by longshore drift
> curved neck of spit where material is deposited
> end of spit rounded by waves
> marshland formed behind spit

2 Use the map you have drawn to explain how a spit is formed. Try to use your own words.

3 Houses have been built at the end of Spurn Head for families of people who work at the lifeboat station. Do you think this is a good idea? Give your reasons.

BUILDING BLOCKS

Should the coastline be saved?

People living on the Holderness coast are worried that they will continue to lose their homes and land to the sea. Although sea defences have been built at four places – Bridlington, Hornsea, Withernsea and now Mappleton – they argue that everyone along the coast deserves to be protected.

G

Sue Earle, owner of a farm just south of Mappleton

> Farmers like me are losing our land and nobody seems to care. It has got worse since they built the new groynes at Mappleton. I used to lose about 1 m of land every year. Now it is more like 10 m. We've had to get rid of our herd of cows. The sea has even taken away our house. The base of the cliffs here used to be protected by the sand that was carried along the coast. Now that they have built the groynes none of the sand can reach us. The waves just pound straight into the cliffs.

H | Four methods of coastal protection

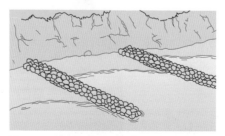

Sea walls give good protection but they are expensive. They deflect the power of the waves back to sea, but this washes the beach away. Wooden groynes are needed to protect the beach. Cost: £7,000 per metre.

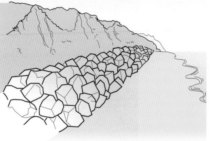

Revetments are like a sea wall but cheaper to build. They break the force of the waves and trap the beach behind them. They don't protect cliffs as well as a sea wall does. Cost: £1,000 per metre.

Beach-feeding replaces the sand which has been lost from the beach. This protects the land or sea wall behind the beach and also looks more natural. Cost: £1,000 per metre.

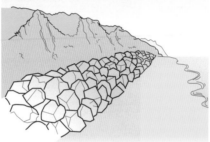

Groynes made of rock slow down the movement of material along the coast and help to build up the beach. This gives more protection to the land behind the beach, but they are very expensive. Cost: £1.5 million per groyne (usually 200 metres apart).

I | The multi-million pound gas plant at Easington is in danger from the sea. Built close to the North Sea, where the gas comes from, its fence is now only a few metres from the cliff edge.

J | In recent years the sea has broken through this road, which joins Spurn Head to the rest of the coast, on a number of occasions. It may not be long before the spit becomes an island.

... or should the sea win?

Geographers now know that protecting one part of the coast can affect places further along the same coastline. Erecting sea defences at Mappleton may lead to greater erosion of cliffs to the south. Problems such as this can only be solved by devising a plan to manage the whole coastline.

One suggestion that has been made is to create a number of artificial bays along the coast by protecting a few fixed points. The obvious places to protect would be the towns – Bridlington, Hornsea and Withernsea – where most people live, as well as Mappleton and Easington which are at risk. The sea would be left to erode the cliffs between these points, forming small bays. Beaches would slowly form in each bay, helping to protect the coast from further erosion. Some material would continue to be transported along the coast to Spurn Head and beyond.

An alternative would be to protect the whole coastline, which would be very expensive. This could also cut off the supply of sand to Spurn Head, which might disappear altogether. Material from the Holderness coast is also transported even further, to East Anglia and even to the Netherlands. These areas, where millions of people live, are now prone to flooding. No one knows what effect protecting the Holderness coast could have on these areas.

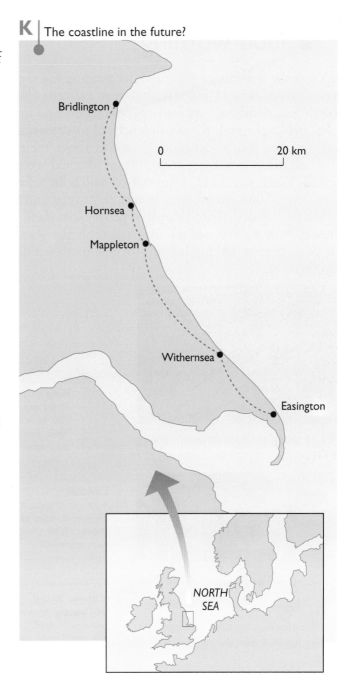

K The coastline in the future?

Activities

1 Study the information on the opposite page.
   Explain why the groynes built at Mappleton
   a) Reduce the erosion of cliffs there
   b) Help to increase erosion further along the coast.

2 Work out the cost of protecting all 60 km of the coastline using each of the different methods shown. If money was not important, which method, or combination of methods, would you choose? Give reasons. What are the arguments against protecting the whole coastline?

Assignment

Write a newspaper report entitled, 'Should the coastline be saved?'
Your report should mention:
- Where the coastline is disappearing
- Why this is happening
- What effects it is having, both good and bad
- What could be done to protect the coast and what the cost might be
- What you think should be done.

You could include maps, diagrams and imaginary interviews with people living or working in the area in your report.

DIGGING DEEPER

2.8 Flood warning!

In 1953 the sea caused the most devastating flood that Britain has ever suffered. On 31 January that year a surge of water in the North Sea, combined with storm conditions and unusually high tides, broke through the sea defences of towns on the east coast of England. Sea levels rose more than 2 m above their normal level, flooding many low-lying areas. Worst affected were parts of East Anglia, Essex and Kent, a quarter of which lie below sea level. Towns were badly damaged, homes destroyed and huge areas of farmland flooded. Three hundred people lost their lives. The flood showed how dangerous and unpredictable the sea can be. It led to the government making big improvements to sea defences around Britain's coast.

A Flooding at Great Yarmouth during 1953

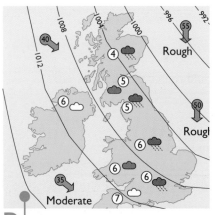

B People rescuing their belongings at Canvey Island, Essex, during the 1953 floods

D Weather map of the UK, 31 January 1953

C The 1953 floods

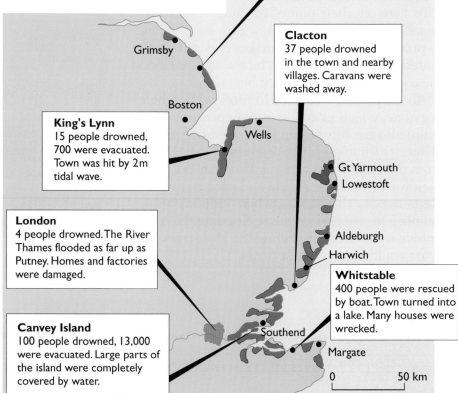

Key
- • Town or city
- ▮ Flooded area

Mablethorpe
5,000 people had to be evacuated from their homes.

Clacton
37 people drowned in the town and nearby villages. Caravans were washed away.

King's Lynn
15 people drowned, 700 were evacuated. Town was hit by 2m tidal wave.

London
4 people drowned. The River Thames flooded as far up as Putney. Homes and factories were damaged.

Canvey Island
100 people drowned, 13,000 were evacuated. Large parts of the island were completely covered by water.

Whitstable
400 people were rescued by boat. Town turned into a lake. Many houses were wrecked.

Grimsby · Boston · Wells · Gt Yarmouth · Lowestoft · Aldeburgh · Harwich · Southend · Margate

0 _____ 50 km

Activities

1 Study the information on this page. Make a table showing the causes and the effects of the 1953 floods.

2 Imagine that you were a resident of a coastal town in East Anglia in 1953. Write a letter to the government suggesting what it should do to reduce the danger of future floods.

Homework

3 Find out about coastal floods that have happened in Britain recently. Most winters bring storms to Britain, often leading to flooding. Collect information from a range of sources, including newspapers and TV reports and the Internet.

Could it happen again?

If scientists' predictions are correct, sea levels around the world are likely to rise by at least half a metre over the next hundred years. This is due to the effect of global warming, which is melting the ice near the North and South Poles. (You can find out more about global warming in *Earthworks 3*.) When this happens, large parts of the British coastline will be at risk from flooding, including many major cities.

The map on the right shows the areas of Britain that are most vulnerable to a rise in sea level. Most of them are close to river estuaries or low-lying coastal marshes. In many places existing sea defences would not be high enough to protect them from expected sea levels. Some of these defences were built after the floods of 1953 and are in need of repair. Even the Thames Barrier near London, completed in 1982, could be overwhelmed by the rise in sea levels that some predict.

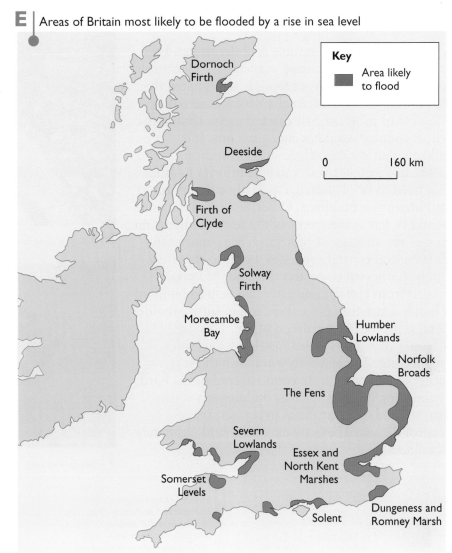

E | Areas of Britain most likely to be flooded by a rise in sea level

Key

Area likely to flood

0   160 km

Dornoch Firth
Deeside
Firth of Clyde
Solway Firth
Morecambe Bay
Humber Lowlands
Norfolk Broads
The Fens
Severn Lowlands
Essex and North Kent Marshes
Somerset Levels
Solent
Dungeness and Romney Marsh

F | The Thames Barrier

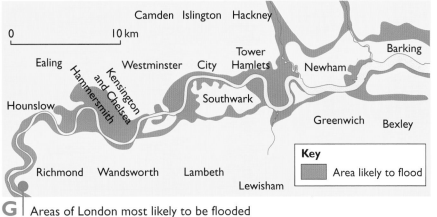

G | Areas of London most likely to be flooded

0   10 km

Camden   Islington   Hackney
Ealing
Westminster   City   Tower Hamlets   Newham   Barking
Hounslow
Hammersmith
Kensington and Chelsea
Southwark
Greenwich   Bexley
Richmond   Wandsworth   Lambeth
Lewisham

Key

Area likely to flood

Activities

1 Use a map of Britain in your atlas to mark and label major cities onto a map of Britain. Shade the areas that are most likely to flood if sea levels rise. Which cities are at greatest risk from flooding?

2 Find a tourist map of central London. Which famous landmarks and tourist attractions in London would be in danger of flooding?

DIGGING DEEPER

Going against the tide?

Much of the British coastline is under threat. Fast-eroding cliffs and low-lying marshes are vulnerable to the expected rise in sea level. It is estimated that 70 per cent of the East Anglian coast is receding. The cost of protecting threatened areas around the whole country would be many billions. It is unlikely that we can afford such protection.

The government wants to give priority to areas that need to be protected, especially cities, ports and important buildings. Other, less valuable, areas would be left at the mercy of the sea. An important part of the strategy of protection is to understand how natural coastal processes work, so that they can be harnessed to protect the land. Material eroded from cliffs in one place can help to build up a beach in another place. Beaches, in turn, provide natural protection for the coastline. This use of natural processes is sometimes known as **soft engineering**. The aim is to work with the sea, rather than against it. In contrast, traditional **hard engineering** projects, such as building sea walls, groynes and other artificial structures, try to control the sea. These are expensive and ultimately as vulnerable to the sea as the coastline itself.

H A sea defence project which has created artificial bays

I Beach-feeding to help maintain the sand level on a beach

Assignment

You are going to produce a plan to protect the coastline of East Anglia.

Look at the map. It shows areas that are at risk from flooding and areas that are being eroded.

Decide which parts of the coast need to be protected. How would they be protected? What would happen to the areas that are not protected? Think about the cost of your plan (the information on page 38 may help).

On a copy of the map, show which areas you would protect. Use symbols to show what methods you would use to protect them. Add a key.

Write a short report to explain your decisions. How did you decide which areas to protect and which to leave?

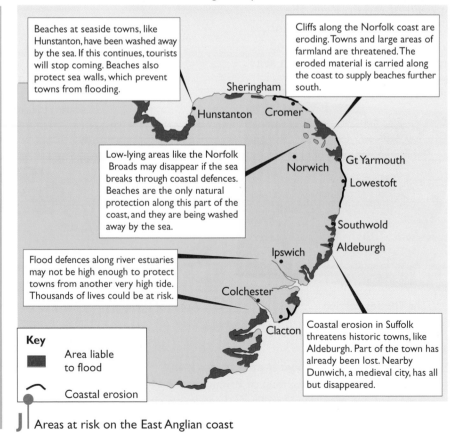

Beaches at seaside towns, like Hunstanton, have been washed away by the sea. If this continues, tourists will stop coming. Beaches also protect sea walls, which prevent towns from flooding.

Cliffs along the Norfolk coast are eroding. Towns and large areas of farmland are threatened. The eroded material is carried along the coast to supply beaches further south.

Low-lying areas like the Norfolk Broads may disappear if the sea breaks through coastal defences. Beaches are the only natural protection along this part of the coast, and they are being washed away by the sea.

Flood defences along river estuaries may not be high enough to protect towns from another very high tide. Thousands of lives could be at risk.

Coastal erosion in Suffolk threatens historic towns, like Aldeburgh. Part of the town has already been lost. Nearby Dunwich, a medieval city, has all but disappeared.

Sheringham
Hunstanton Cromer
Norwich Gt Yarmouth
Lowestoft
Ipswich Southwold
Aldeburgh
Colchester
Clacton

Key
■ Area liable to flood
⌐ Coastal erosion

J Areas at risk on the East Anglian coast

Commuters in London

London is the capital city of the United Kingdom. It is a very large **settlement**. Settlements are places where people live. Over half the people in the world today live in cities.

- Where do you think these people are going? Where might they live?
- What do you imagine they are thinking?
- How would you feel about living or working here?
- Why do people live in cities?

GROUNDWORK

3.1 **W**ho needs neighbours?

You probably live in an **urban** area – a built-up area which is part of a town or city. This is not just a guess! Nine out of every ten people in Britain live in a town or city. This makes it one of the most urbanised countries in the world.

Two hundred years ago the situation was quite different. At that time most people lived in villages in **rural** areas, in the countryside. This is still the case in some countries today.

People usually move to cities to find jobs and for a better quality of life. But they don't always find these. Some cities have high levels of unemployment, crime and pollution.

A *Emmerdale*, set in the Yorkshire Dales, a rural area

Activities

1 Look at the two photos. They are from two well-known TV soap operas: *Emmerdale* and *EastEnders*.

   What would you like or dislike about living in each of these places?

2 Read the list of features in the box below. Are they features of urban or rural areas? Sort them into two lists, one to describe each type of area.

> tall buildings   fields   trees
> shopping centres
> traffic jams   concrete
> parks   pollution   villages
> housing estates   farms
> factories   litter   fresh air
> isolated buildings   few people
> open space   narrow lanes
> entertainment   many people

Homework

3 Watch an episode of a TV soap opera. Look for any other features of an urban area or a rural area. Add these features to your list.

   Think about the area where you live. Which type of area is it most like? What do you like or dislike about living there?

B *EastEnders*, set in London, an urban area

Neighbours is another popular TV soap opera set in the city of Melbourne, Australia. Because it is near the edge of the city, the area is neither really urban nor really rural. This type of place is called **suburban**. Many people have moved out from city centres to live in suburban areas. This has happened in Britain as well as in Australia. Some villages in rural areas, close to cities, are also growing to be more like suburbs. The difference between urban and rural is getting smaller.

C *Neighbours*, set in the suburbs of Melbourne

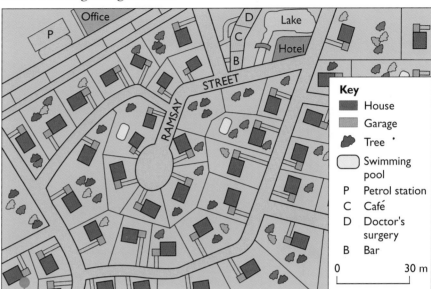

D The area of Melbourne where *Neighbours* is set

Hi! What are you doing after school? Do you fancy coming round to my place for a swim?

Er – well, I don't mean to be rude, but I've already arranged to do my geography homework. Maybe some other day, OK?

Activities

1 Study the information on this page. List the features of a suburban area.

   What are the advantages of living in an area like this? Can you think of any disadvantages?

2 Write your own scene for an episode of *Neighbours*. Include information in your story describing life in a suburban area. If you often watch *Neighbours*, you can choose characters from the soap; if not, make up your own characters. Locate the scene on a copy of the map.

3 Complete an environmental quality chart for each of the three places in the TV soaps. Choose your own words to write on the chart, or look back to page 12. Work out an environmental quality score for each place.

	Very	**Rather**	**Neither/Nor**	**Rather**	**Very**	
Negative words	−2	−1	0	+1	+2	**Positive words**

In which type of place would you most like to live? Give your reasons.

FRAMEWORK

3.2 Settlement sites

The place where a settlement is built is its **site**. Most settlements in Britain date back hundreds, or even thousands, of years to the times of the Celts, Romans, Saxons and Vikings. The sites they chose depended on a number of natural features, including the shape of the land, the climate and what resources were available. The settlements that grew were those that had the best sites.

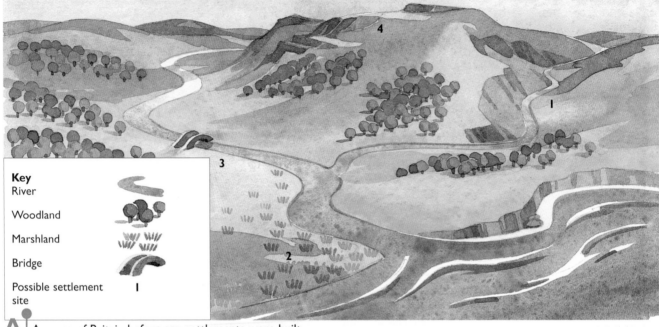

Key
River

Woodland

Marshland

Bridge

Possible settlement site I

A | An area of Britain before any settlements were built

Activities

1 Look at drawing A. It shows an area in Britain before settlements had been built. 1, 2, 3 and 4 are possible sites for a settlement. What is the only feature in the drawing made by humans?

2 Read the list of natural features in the table on the right. These are what early settlers looked for when choosing a site.
   On a copy of the table, tick the boxes for the natural features which each site has. Which is the best site for a settlement? Give reasons.
   Which site might be preferred by people who were:
   a) Farmers
   b) Local warriors
   c) Invaders from another country?

Natural feature Site	1	2	3	4
Water supply – close to river for drinking water				
Defence – hilltop sites have good views and are easy to defend				
Building material – close to woodland or rocky hillside				
Farmland – flat land usually has good soil for growing crops				
Fuel – wood needed to burn for warmth and cooking				
Flood prevention – sites away from rivers and marshland are safer				
Rivers – provide transport but must be narrow enough to bridge				
Shelter – close to steep slopes or woodland				

... and shapes

If you look at a map, you will notice that all settlements have different shapes. Their shape is often influenced by the same natural features as affect the site of the settlement.

In lowland parts of Britain it is common to find **nucleated settlements,** where buildings are grouped together. Settlements with this shape often grew around a road junction or river crossing. Sometimes a wall was built around the settlement for protection. In upland areas it is more common to find **dispersed settlements,** where buildings are spread further apart. Here people needed more land to grow their crops or graze animals. Their position gave them better natural protection. **Linear settlements** are more likely to be found along valley bottoms or close to a road.

B Warkworth, Northumberland

C Isle of Skye, Scotland

Activities

1 Look at photos B, C and D. They show settlements with different shapes. Match each photo with one of the three shapes – nucleated, dispersed or linear. Write a sentence to describe the shape of the settlement in each photo.

2 The map shows the area in drawing A. Choose the most likely site for each of the three types of settlement.

On a large copy of the map, draw each of the settlements at the sites you have chosen. Make each one the correct shape. Add roads to the map to link the settlements. Think about the best route for each road.

Use the list of natural features on the opposite page to help you decide which settlement on your map would be most likely to grow. Explain why.

Homework

3 Find out more about the settlement that you live in. Is it a village, a town or part of a large city? What site was the settlement built on? Why was that site chosen? What shape is the settlement? When did people start living there? How has it grown?

D Ironbridge, Shropshire

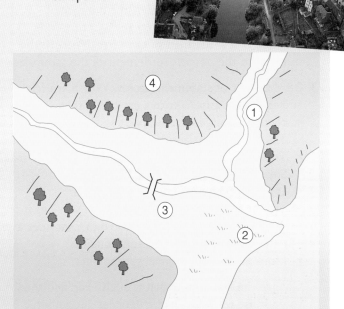

FRAMEWORK

3.3 Settlement size

Settlements also vary greatly in size. Their size can affect the type of **shops** and **services** they provide. Shops sell goods, while services, such as schools and leisure centres, are provided to meet people's needs. The smallest settlements are **hamlets**, which consist of a few houses and usually have no shops or services. Villages are larger and often have a few shops and services, such as a post office or pub. Settlements that have grown into towns or cities provide a much greater range of shops and services. In general, the larger the settlement the more it provides. The chart shows some of the shops and services you might expect to find in each type of settlement.

Settlement	Shops and services
Hamlet	None
Village	Post office, pub, church, general store, primary school
Town	All of the above, plus supermarket, many shops, banks, health centre, leisure centre, secondary school, train and/or bus station
City	All of the above, plus large shopping centre with specialist shops, many supermarkets, cathedral, hospital, university, museums, theatre, sports stadium

Activities

1   Look at map A, which shows settlements around York and Hull in East Yorkshire.

2   Draw a table like the one below.

Type of settlement	How many on map?	Example	Distance apart	Population range	Likely shops and services
Village		South Cave			

To complete your table, count the number of settlements of each size on map A. Choose one example of a settlement of each size. Measure the distance to the nearest settlement of the same size.

3   Read the list of statements below. Which are true and which are false? Write a list of the true statements, entitled 'Rules about settlements'.
   • There are more large settlements than small ones.
   • There are more small settlements than large ones.
   • Smaller settlements are closer together.
   • Larger settlements are closer together.
   • The larger the settlement the more services it provides.
   • The smaller the settlement the more services it provides.
   • More people live in large settlements.
   • More people live in small settlements.

Change the statements that are false and add them to your list, to make eight true rules altogether.

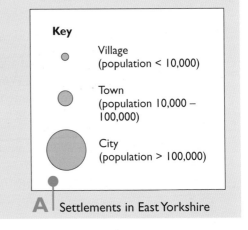

Key

● Village (population < 10,000)

● Town (population 10,000 – 100,000)

● City (population > 100,000)

A Settlements in East Yorkshire

... *and functions*

Most settlements provide services but, as they grow, some settlements have developed other **functions**.

Some of the earliest settlements grew as **defensive towns**, to protect their inhabitants against attacks from enemies. Others grew as **market towns**, where farmers and people from neighbouring settlements would come to buy and sell goods. Settlements built near rivers or the coast were often **ports**, where ships were able to bring in goods from other places and take other goods away. Later, particularly during the 19th century in Britain, other settlements grew into **industrial towns** or holiday **resorts**.

Many settlements have changed their function over time. For example, many villages that were once fishing ports have now turned into holiday resorts.

B | Hull

C | Beverley

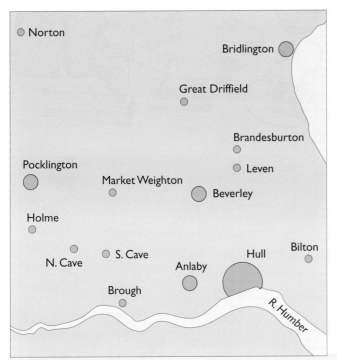

D | Bridlington

Activities

1 Look at photos B, C and D. Identify the function of each of the settlements. Locate each settlement on map A. Write a sentence to describe the location of each settlement. In each case, explain why its location is well suited to its function.

2 In your atlas find a map of the area shown in map A. Compare the pattern of settlements with the rivers and hills in the area. What do you notice? Where are most settlements found?

Where are fewest settlements found?

Explain the pattern of settlements that you can see on the map.

Homework

3 Find out the original function of your own settlement. Has its function changed? How? What are its functions now?

Draw a shield for your settlement, decorated with symbols to illustrate its functions today.

FRAMEWORK

3.4 **S**hops and services

In smaller settlements, shops and services are usually located at the centre, where they are easy for most people to reach. Larger settlements are likely to have more than one shopping centre. In recent years many of these have been built out of town. People may visit different centres for different types of goods and services. Things that people buy frequently, such as food or newspapers, are called **convenience** or **low-order goods**. These can usually be bought at a local shopping centre or a supermarket. Things that people buy less often such as clothes or furniture, are called **comparison** or **high-order goods**. These are bought at large shopping centres, in the city centre or out of town.

Activities

1 Look at the goods shown in the picture on the right. Sort them into two groups – low-order goods and high-order goods. Write two separate shopping lists.

2 Plan a visit to the shopping centre shown in the map below. Decide which shops you need to visit for the items on your two lists. Are there any goods that you will not be able to buy?

   Work out the best route to take around the shopping centre. Think about where you would get your money, which goods would be heavy to carry, and how you would travel home.

A | Shopping goods

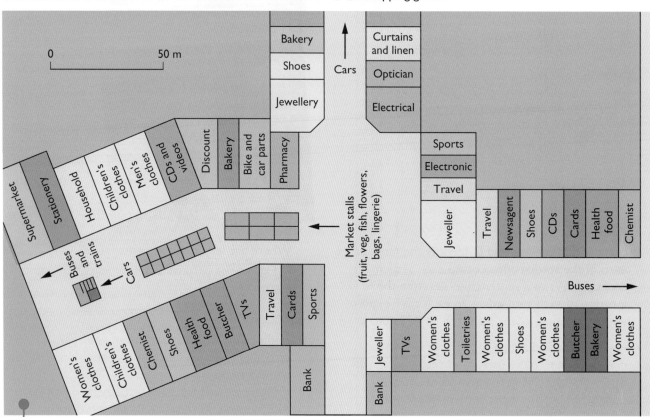

B | A shopping centre

C | Princess Quay shopping centre in Hull

A group of pupils visited a city shopping centre to investigate the shopping habits of the people who go there. This is a copy of the results of their shopping survey.

SHOPPING SURVEY

1 How often do you shop here?

Every day	4
Once a week, or more	12
Once a month, or more	56
Less than once a month	28

2 How far do you travel to come here?

Less than 1 mile	9
Between 1 and 2 miles	24
Between 2 and 5 miles	47
More than 5 miles	20

3 How do you travel here?

On foot	3
By car	62
By train or bus	26
Other	9

4 What is the main thing you come here to buy?

Food	8
Clothes or shoes	54
Large household goods	17
Other	21

Local investigation

How do the shopping habits of people who use a local shopping centre compare with those who use a city centre?

Work in a group. Do a shopping survey at your local shopping centre. You can use a copy of the shopping survey sheet above, or make up your own. Work with a partner.

Each pair will need: a copy of the survey sheet, a clipboard, a pencil.

At the shopping centre:

• Interview shoppers. Decide how many shoppers each pair in the group will interview (try to do 100 between the whole group). Include as many types of people as you can, to represent all the shoppers at the centre.

• Mark the correct box beside the answer each shopper gives. Use the same sheet for all your interviews.

In the classroom:

• Share all the answers with the other members of your group. Count the total number of marks for each answer.

• Think of ways to display the results using suitable graphs or diagrams and draw these.

 You could record your results on a database, using a computer and a graph-drawing package to draw your graphs.

• Describe the graphs and diagrams that you have drawn and explain what they show.

• Compare the results of the survey at your local shopping centre with a city shopping centre. You can use the results on this page or investigate the city centre nearest to you. Write four paragraphs to compare:
  – How often people shop there
  – How they travel there
  – How far they travel to get there
  – What they buy there.

BUILDING BLOCKS

In this Building Block you will look at historical evidence of London's growth to compare past and present.

3.5 **W**hy did London grow?

> I was in the Roman army of the Emperor Claudius, which conquered Britain in AD 43. We landed in the south-east of the country after we had crossed the sea from Gaul (France). We marched north, seizing control from the local tribes. The main obstacle was the River Thames which, towards the sea, was too wide to cross, and its banks too marshy to build a bridge. Eventually we found a place to build a bridge as close to the sea as possible. To begin with, it was just a crossing point to help our army reach other parts of the country. But the Britons attacked and we had to defend the bridge. Soldiers built a camp around the bridge. Soon there were other people living there and it grew into a city. We called it Londinium. The city became the main port in Britain with boats coming to and from Rome. It was also the centre of our road network, linking all the cities we built. Within 50 years, Londinium was the capital city of Britain.

gate and road from city   fort
amphitheatre

forum and basilica

River Thames   Governor's palace

Southwark   bridge   port   city wall

A Roman London

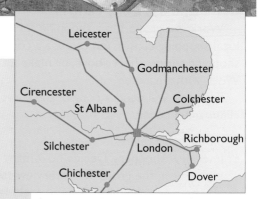

Activities

1 Look at the Roman soldier's explanation and the drawing of Roman London (Londinium). List all the features that led to the development of this settlement.

 London was the **lowest bridging point** on the River Thames. Explain what you think this means.

2 Draw a sketch map to show the main features of the drawing. Label the features that show the advantages of this site for a settlement, for example good flat land for building and farming.

3 Write a letter from the commander of the Roman army in Britain to the Emperor Claudius, asking him for money and more soldiers to build a city. Persuade the Emperor that this is a good place for a capital city.

B Covent Garden Market originally opened in 1670. It sold fruit and vegetables for the growing population of London. Eventually it became too congested and in 1970 a new market was built further from the centre. Covent Garden now sells clothes and souvenirs.

C The Tower of London was built by William the Conqueror in 1066. It was built to defend London from invaders, but is now a tourist attraction. In the background is the City of London where many large banks and other companies have their headquarters.

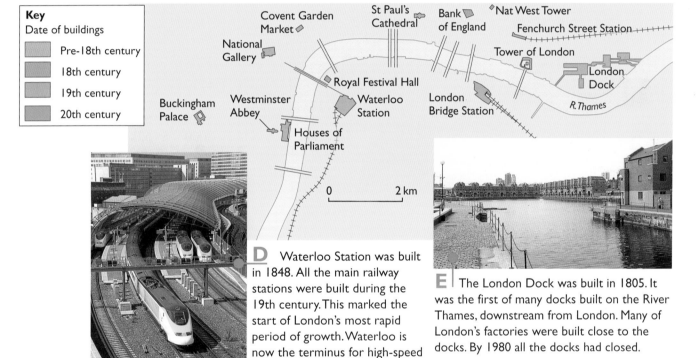

Key
Date of buildings

- Pre-18th century
- 18th century
- 19th century
- 20th century

Covent Garden Market
National Gallery
St Paul's Cathedral
Bank of England
Nat West Tower
Fenchurch Street Station
Tower of London
London Dock
Royal Festival Hall
Buckingham Palace
Westminster Abbey
Waterloo Station
London Bridge Station
R. Thames
Houses of Parliament

0   2 km

D Waterloo Station was built in 1848. All the main railway stations were built during the 19th century. This marked the start of London's most rapid period of growth. Waterloo is now the terminus for high-speed trains to Paris and Brussels.

E The London Dock was built in 1805. It was the first of many docks built on the River Thames, downstream from London. Many of London's factories were built close to the docks. By 1980 all the docks had closed.

Activities

1 Study all the information on these two pages. What can you tell about London's many different functions?

Draw a table like the one below listing all the functions that London has had. Give evidence for each of these functions. State whether or not it still has each function. One has been started for you.

Function	Evidence	Does it still have this function?
Port	the docks	

When we built a bridge I never imagined that it would end up like this!

2 If a Roman soldier were to return to London today he might be amazed to see how it has grown.

Imagine the conversation that you might have with him. Suggest why London has grown so much since Roman times. Mention all its functions and say how these have changed.

How has London changed?

It was after the mid-19th century that London grew most rapidly. In 1800 places like Hampstead were villages well outside the built-up area of London. By 1900, mainly because of the new railway network, they had become part of a huge urban area. Today, Hampstead is a suburb quite close to central London – only ten minutes away on the Underground. London is now described as a **conurbation** – a very large urban area into which many separate settlements have merged.

F The view from Hampstead, shown in Constable's painting of 1834

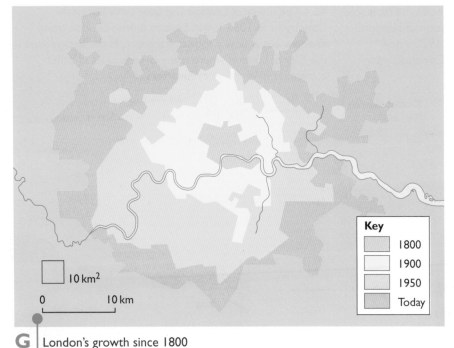

Key
- 1800
- 1900
- 1950
- Today

10 km²

0   10 km

G London's growth since 1800

1800	1,000,000
1850	3,000,000
1900	6,500,000
1950	8,000,000
2000	6,000,000 (estimated)

H Population change in London

I The view from Hampstead today

Activities

1 Look at map G, which shows the growth of London since 1800.

 Estimate the area of London at each of the four dates shown on the key. To do this accurately, draw a **grid** on tracing paper using the 10 km² shown on the scale. Place it over the map. Count the number of squares which London covered at each date.

 Draw a bar graph to show London's growth. Use a grid like the top one here.

1800	1850	1900	1950	2000

1800	1850	1900	1950	2000

2 Look at table H, which shows the change of population in London since 1800. Draw a line graph to show London's population change. Use a grid like the bottom one here.

Assignment

Write an extract for a history book about the growth of London.

 Compare London as it was at the beginning of the 19th century with London today. Use all the information from this investigation. Include each of these words in your extract:

| urban   village   railway |
| conurbation   suburb   rural |

In this Building Block you will use a map and photos to compare services in settlements of different sizes.

York

3.6 What services can you find?

People in cities may dream of living in a village in the country. They want to leave the stress, noise and pollution of urban life. However, they would also find themselves much further away from services that they need. In the city these may be just down the road.

Activities

1 Look at the photos on this page. They show some settlements near York. What types of shops and services can you see in each photo?

2 Find each settlement on the 1:50,000 OS map extract on the next page. Give the four-figure grid reference for each settlement.

3 Read the lists of shops and services that can be found in each settlement. Can you find any of the services on the map? Use the key below to help you.

╪ ╪ +	Church	☎	Telephone
		▬	Station
		⬥	Bus station
P	Post office		
PH	Public house	⬠	Sch

Name the services that can be found at these six-figure references. Which settlement are they in?

677 552   668 525   630 512   595 517

How many types of services can you find in York? Give a six-figure grid reference for one example of each type of service you can find.

A | Warthill

Services: church   pub phone   primary school

B | Dunnington

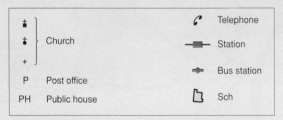

Shops and services: 2 churches   2 pubs phone   2 supermarkets   post office newsagent   butcher   chemist   florist hair salon   estate agent   off-licence doctor   dentist   primary school

C | Haxby

Shops and services: 5 estate agents   4 banks 3 pubs   3 supermarkets   3 chemists   3 clothes shops 2 churches   2 take-away restaurants   2 stationers 2 greengrocers   2 hair salons   2 vets   2 newsagents 2 butchers   2 restaurants   post office   optician dry cleaner   off-licence   insurance agent   baker electrical shop   DIY shop   travel agent picture framer   carpet shop   antique shop health centre   doctor   dentist   ambulance station garage   solicitor   2 primary schools

BUILDING BLOCKS

D York

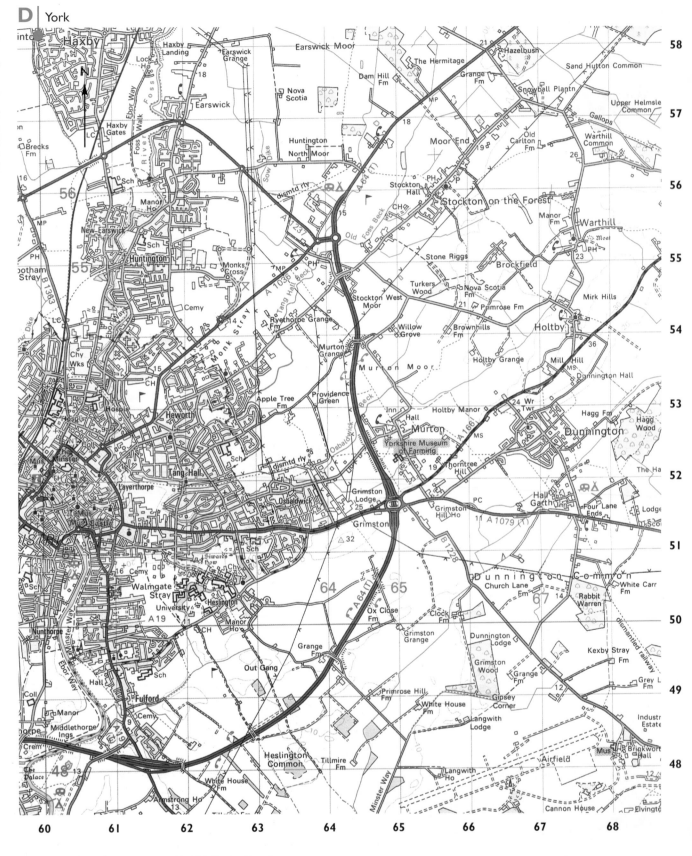

Reproduced from the 1994 1:50,000 Ordnance Survey map
of York by permission of the Controller of HMSO © Crown
Copyright

What difference does size make?

Activities

1 Look at table E. It shows the population of four of the settlements on the map.

E

Settlement	Population
Dunnington	3,000
Haxby	9,400
Warthill	250
York	98,000

Rank the settlements in order of population. Draw a bar chart of population with the bars in that order.

2 From the map, estimate the size of each settlement. (Each square on the map is 1 km^2.)

Rank the settlements in order of their size. Draw a bar chart of settlement size with the bars in that order.

Compare the two bar charts. Explain the link between the population and the size of settlements.

3 Count the total number of shops and services found in Warthill, Dunnington and Haxby (listed on page 55). Rank the three settlements in order of the number of shops and services. Draw a bar chart of the number of shops and services with the bars in that order.

F York city centre

Compare all the bar charts. Explain the link between the number of shops and services a settlement has and its size. How many services would you expect to find in York?

Think of shops and services that you may find in York and cannot find in the smaller settlements.

4 Imagine that you live in York. You are thinking of moving away from the city to a village, like Warthill. For each of the goods and services in the box below:

> a pub   a primary school   a newspaper   a doctor
> food   petrol   a secondary school   a train station

a) Find out where you would have to go if you moved.
b) Measure on the map how far you would have to travel.

Think about the advantages and disadvantages of living in a village like Warthill. Decide whether or not it would be a good idea to move from York to Warthill.

G Monk's Cross shopping centre outside York

Assignment

In the last few years two new out-of-town shopping centres have opened to the north of York. One is at Clifton Moor (59 55) and the other at Monk's Cross (62 54).

Suggest how this might affect the shops and services in the four settlements you have looked at on the map, and what differences this may make to the shopping habits of people living there.

Either: Plan an investigation in the area on the map, to find out whether or not your ideas are correct.

Or: Plan and carry out a local investigation to find out what impact a new shopping centre has had on your own area.

BUILDING BLOCKS

In this Building Block you will find out what Milton Keynes is like and plan your own **new town**.

3.7 What is Milton Keynes like?

Claire

> I live in a new town called Milton Keynes.
> It is the largest new town in Britain and it was also the last one to be built. They didn't start to build it until 1970. Until then there were just trees and cows and a few villages around here.
> Actually, it's more of a city than a town – we've got a huge shopping centre with all the main chain stores like John Lewis and Marks & Spencer. But sometimes you would think you were still living in the country. There are lots of parks and lakes, and I can cycle to the town centre without even having to cross a main road!

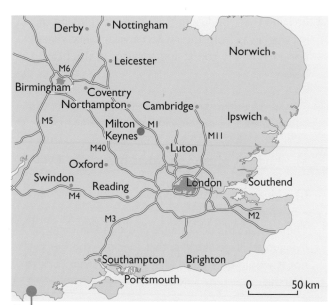

A | Location of Milton Keynes

B | An aerial view of Milton Keynes today

Activities

1 Look at map A, which shows the location of Milton Keynes. Measure the distance by road from Milton Keynes to London and Birmingham. Which motorway is it close to?

   Suggest why this may be a good location for a new town.

2 Look at map C, which shows the area of Milton Keynes as it was before building began in 1969. Name the settlements that were already there.

   Describe the site on which Milton Keynes was built. What features formed the boundary of the new town?

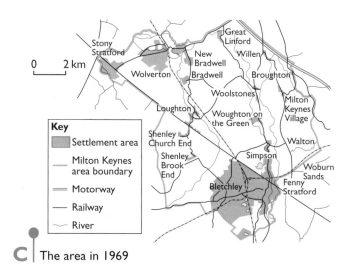

Key

- Settlement area
- Milton Keynes area boundary
- Motorway
- Railway
- River

C | The area in 1969

What makes it different?

Since 1970 Milton Keynes has been the fastest-growing urban area in Britain. There are now about 200,000 people living there. Like other new towns, it was carefully planned before it was built. The plan contained a good balance of housing and employment, so that people would not have to travel elsewhere for work. It was also designed so that it would provide shops and services to meet people's needs.

D | How Milton Keynes compares with the rest of the UK

	Milton Keynes (%)	**UK (%)**
Population under 16	25	21
Population over 65	10	16
Population in skilled/ professional jobs	29	26
Population unemployed	5	7

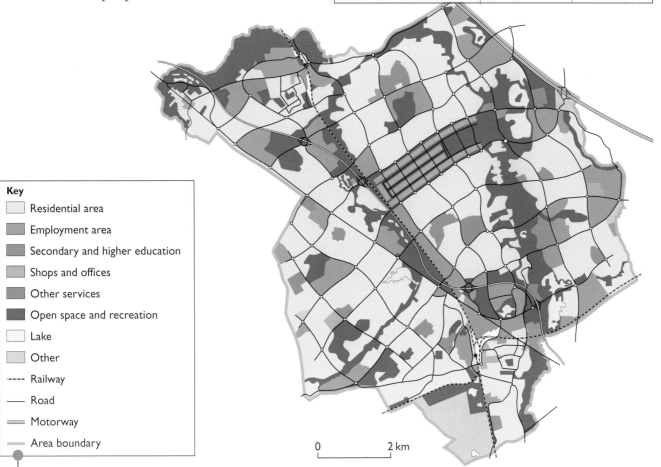

Key
- ▢ Residential area
- ▢ Employment area
- ▢ Secondary and higher education
- ▢ Shops and offices
- ▢ Other services
- ▢ Open space and recreation
- ▢ Lake
- ▢ Other
- ---- Railway
- — Road
- ═══ Motorway
- — Area boundary

0   2 km

E | Land use in Milton Keynes

Activities

1 Look at table D, which compares the population of Milton Keynes with the rest of the UK population. Write four sentences to describe what the table shows.

2 Look at map E, which shows how the land in Milton Keynes is used. Estimate what percentage of the total area each land use covers. Rank the land uses in order of the area they cover.

Homework

3 On a copy of a map of your local area, colour the land uses that you find. (You may have to use an aerial photo or walk around the area in groups to do this.) Rank the land uses in order of the area they cover.

Compare Milton Keynes with your own area. What differences or similarities do you notice? Which land uses seem to be more important in Milton Keynes and which seem to be more important in your area?

New service solutions?

The local area I live in is Great Linford. Milton Keynes is divided into many local areas. Each one has most of the basic services that people need so they are more **accessible**. Great Linford is built around the old village, so it isn't all new. Our church is over 600 years old! At the moment I go to Great Linford Combined School. It is a primary school and middle school joined together. When I go into Year 8 I'll go to Stantonbury Campus, which is one of the biggest schools in the country. It's quite close to here, so I'll still be able to cycle to school.

F Great Linford

G Houses in Great Linford

KEY

	Education areas		●	Bus stop
	Open space and recreation		☲	Picnic site
■ ✉	Post box, Post office		X	Taxi rank
	Telephone call box		P	Car park
⊕	Health centre, clinic or surgery		T	Toilet
	Playground		†	Church

H Great Linford local centre

Activities

1 Claire lives in Granes End. Find it on map F. List all the services she would be able to find in Great Linford.

 Describe the best route for Claire to go to school. How far does she have to cycle?

Homework

2 Find out from a map of your own local area how far you would have to walk or cycle to each of these services. Mark each of these services on a map of your area.

 Compare Great Linford with your own local area. Which area provides the most services? How easy are they to reach?

... or new problems?

Milton Keynes is unlike any other town or city in Britain. Most British cities have a **radial** road system where all roads lead to the city centre, like spokes in a wheel. This often leads to traffic congestion. Milton Keynes was planned on a **grid** system, more like some American cities. Homes and jobs are spread more evenly around the city and can be reached quickly by car. However, Milton Keynes does have a city centre where all the large shops are found. It also has a number of larger district centres, which provide some of the shops and services that cannot be found at local centres. There is less public transport in Milton Keynes than in most towns, so each centre has been designed with plenty of car parks for people to leave their cars.

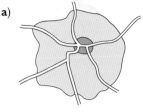

a)

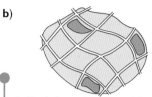

b)

I **a)** Radial road system **b)** Grid road system

K Milton Keynes city centre

Key

▨ Central Milton Keynes
■ District centre
● Major local centre
• Minor local centre
--- Area boundary

0   2 km

J Service centres in Milton Keynes

Activities

1 Look at map J, which shows the shop and service centres in Milton Keynes. Count the number of centres of each size.
Suggest what shops and services you might find at each type of centre.

2 Think about shopping centres in your own town or city. Divide them into different types. Which type of centre is most common? What goods or services do you get at each type of centre?

3 In most towns and cities, public transport travels to and from the centre along radial routes. Why do you think it is difficult to plan public transport in Milton Keynes? Give your reasons for your answer.
If Milton Keynes was being planned today, do you think it would be planned in the same way? Give reasons for your answer.

Assignment

You are going to plan your own new town.

Choose a name for the town and decide how many people would live there. How big would it be? What services would it provide?

Include these features in your plan:

• A transport network, which could include roads, bus routes, railways, etc.

• Different land uses and a map with a key to show how each area would be used.

Write a report to describe your town. Explain why you have planned it this way.

3.8 The urban explosion

Fifty years ago London was the world's second largest city. At that time, most of the largest cities were in Europe and North America. Today the situation has changed. Over half the world's population now live in cities. London is no longer even in the top ten. The fastest-growing cities are mainly in Asia, Africa and South America. Here, thousands of people every day move from the countryside into the cities in search of work and a home. Most go to the **shanty towns** – areas around the city where people build their own homes on empty land from whatever material they can find. Millions of people live in such areas, which often lack safe drinking water, electricity and sanitation.

In Europe and North America, cities are no longer growing rapidly but they too have their problems. Old city centres have declined and face high levels of unemployment and crime. The shortage of decent housing means they also have growing numbers of people without a proper home.

A São Paulo, one of the world's fastest-growing cities

B The world's largest cities today

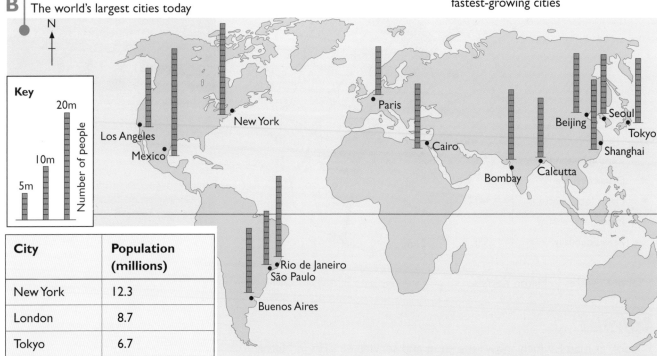

City	Population (millions)
New York	12.3
London	8.7
Tokyo	6.7
Paris	5.4
Shanghai	5.3
Buenos Aires	5.0
Chicago	4.9
Moscow	4.8
Calcutta	4.4
Los Angeles	4.0

C The world's largest cities in 1950

Activities

1 Look at map B. Use the vertical scale on the map to work out the population of each city. Rank the cities in order of their population. Where are most of the largest cities today?

2 Look at table C, which shows the population of the world's largest cities in 1950. Find each city on a world map in an atlas. Where were the largest cities in 1950?
   Compare the location of the largest cities today with 1950.

. . . and its fall-out

D | Homeless person in London

Morag was born in Glasgow, one of five children. Her family lived in a three-bedroomed flat in an old tenement block. Space was always tight, but as the children grew up things got worse. Everyone wanted their own space. Morag had several rows with her parents and, when the tension grew too much to bear, she left home. She was just 15.

She travelled to London, because she had a cousin there. She had always wanted to explore the capital. At first, this went well. Morag found a part-time job in a restaurant and went to college to take the exams that she had missed at school. Then her cousin left the flat to move in with her boyfriend. Morag had to leave because she couldn't afford to pay the rent on her own. She had no choice but to live on the street. Her health and appearance suffered. She lost her job in the restaurant and her college attendance got worse.

Now, she's glad to be staying at a hostel, even though she has to share a room with other homeless teenagers. Eventually, she'd like a place of her own, but flats in London are expensive and first she has to find a well-paid job.

Alfonso lives in São Paulo, the largest city in Brazil. He was born there 12 years ago, after his family had migrated from the countryside. They were very poor and lived in a 'favela' – a shanty town on the outskirts of São Paulo.

From as young as he can remember, Alfonso helped his parents when they went to work in the city centre. They roasted corn to sell to passers-by. None of the children in the family went to school – they all needed to earn money to support themselves. By the time he was nine, Alfonso worked with his older brother. They did whatever jobs would pay – shoe-shining, windscreen-washing, newspaper selling – and when they couldn't earn enough money they would steal. Sometimes they did not go home, either because they were tired, or because they had no money to bring back. They began to sleep in the street and soon realised they were not alone. There were hundreds of other 'street children' in São Paulo. Today they have learnt to survive apart from their family. Even though it is a dangerous place, the city has become their home.

E | Street children in São Paulo, Brazil

Activity

Read the accounts of two homeless young people in different cities. In each case, list the reasons for being homeless. Are there any similarities? What are the differences?

Assignment

Prepare a TV programme about homelessness. Base your programme around real people, including the two people that you have read about here. Explain the reasons for homelessness, and suggest how it can be reduced.

Before you begin it may help to play the game on the next page. You could also find out more about homelessness in Britain and in other parts of the world, by using newspaper and magazine articles and writing to or e-mailing organisations involved in working with homeless people.

Homeless in the city

It is not unusual to be homeless. Around one-third of the world's population either have no home, or live in 'homes' that lack basic services and are bad for their health. In Britain in 1996 there were 122,000 homeless families – about 350,000 people. There may be many more people in Britain without a home who are not listed as homeless, because they live with friends or in overcrowded households.

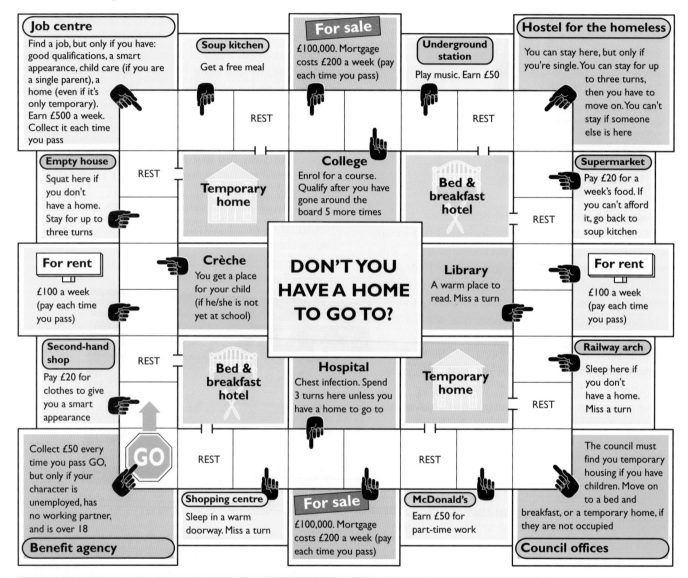

Job centre
Find a job, but only if you have: good qualifications, a smart appearance, child care (if you are a single parent), a home (even if it's only temporary). Earn £500 a week. Collect it each time you pass

Soup kitchen
Get a free meal

REST

For sale
£100,000. Mortgage costs £200 a week (pay each time you pass)

Underground station
Play music. Earn £50

REST

Hostel for the homeless
You can stay here, but only if you're single. You can stay for up to three turns, then you have to move on. You can't stay if someone else is here

Empty house
Squat here if you don't have a home. Stay for up to three turns

REST

Temporary home

College
Enrol for a course. Qualify after you have gone around the board 5 more times

Bed & breakfast hotel

Supermarket
Pay £20 for a week's food. If you can't afford it, go back to soup kitchen

REST

For rent
£100 a week (pay each time you pass)

Crèche
You get a place for your child (if he/she is not yet at school)

DON'T YOU HAVE A HOME TO GO TO?

Library
A warm place to read. Miss a turn

For rent
£100 a week (pay each time you pass)

Second-hand shop
Pay £20 for clothes to give you a smart appearance

REST

Bed & breakfast hotel

Hospital
Chest infection. Spend 3 turns here unless you have a home to go to

Temporary home

REST

Railway arch
Sleep here if you don't have a home. Miss a turn

Benefit agency
Collect £50 every time you pass GO, but only if your character is unemployed, has no working partner, and is over 18

GO

REST

Shopping centre
Sleep in a warm doorway. Miss a turn

For sale
£100,000. Mortgage costs £200 a week (pay each time you pass)

REST

McDonald's
Earn £50 for part-time work

Council offices
The council must find you temporary housing if you have children. Move on to a bed and breakfast, or a temporary home, if they are not occupied

Activity

Play the game in groups of 4–6. One player will be the banker, who looks after the money.

You will need: a dice, a character card, a token and an 'occupied sign' for each player. You will also need to make pretend money (lots of £10, £20 and £50 notes) for the bank. Players start with no money!

Your aim is to find a permanent home – either 'For rent' or 'For sale' – and keep it until the end of the game. Start on GO. Take turns to roll the dice.

Move your token clockwise. Follow the instructions next to each square. You can only occupy a 'For sale or 'For rent' property if you have enough money. You can only get to 'Bed & breakfast' or 'Temporary home' if you get sent there from the Council offices.

When you find a temporary or permanent home, place your 'Occupied' sign on your home. No one else can live there while it is yours. You continue to move around the board. Continue playing until all the 'For sale' or 'For rent' homes are occupied

A muddy scene at Glastonbury open-air festival after days of heavy rain

Fortunately, we don't get this sort of **weather** too often. Weather is the condition of the **atmosphere**, or air around us, from day to day.

- At what time of year do you think the photo was taken?
- How can you tell?
- What do you expect the weather to be like at this time of year?
- Why is weather so unpredictable?

GROUNDWORK

Here is the weather forecast...

A A weather satellite in orbit around the Earth

Every day, on the TV and on radio, you can hear the weather forecast. It tells you what the weather will be like for the next 24 hours. Sometimes, it even forecasts the weather a few days ahead. In the UK weather forecasting is difficult because the weather changes so much from day to day.

People who study the weather are called **meteorologists**. In Britain our weather forecasts come from the **Meteorological Office** (or Met. Office for short). Nowadays meteorology is very scientific. All around the country, from the Scilly Isles to Shetland, weather observations are taken every hour. These are backed up by hundreds of other observations taken out at sea, and by weather balloons in the air and weather satellites in space. Computers build up a picture of the weather from all this information. This is used by skilled meteorologists to make their forecasts.

B A TV weather forecaster

Activities

1 Look at B. Can you recognise all the symbols on the weather map? Match each of the weather symbols with one type of weather in the box below.

> sun   sunny spells   clouds   rain
> snow   windy

Draw your own key to the weather map.
Describe the weather, shown on the map, for the part of Britain where you live.

2 Write a short script for the weather forecaster to read, to give the weather forecast shown on the map. Mention each part of the country in your script.

C | Fishing in the North Sea

We all depend on the weather forecast, even if only to help us decide what to wear. With the help of modern technology, weather forecasts today are usually quite accurate. This is important to those people whose jobs, or even whose safety, can be affected by the weather.

D | Cricket at Lord's, in London

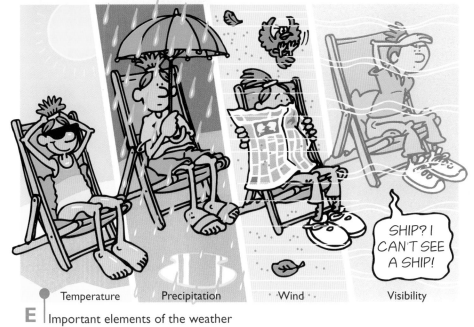

SHIP? I CAN'T SEE A SHIP!

Temperature   Precipitation   Wind   Visibility

E | Important elements of the weather

F | Selling ice-creams at Blackpool

Activities

1   Match each element of the weather in drawing E with the correct meaning below.
   - Movement of the air
   - Water in the air which falls to the ground as rain, snow, sleet or hail
   - A measure of how hot or cold the air is
   - The distance through the air that you can see

   Write each word with the correct meaning beside it.

2   Look at the photos. Explain how the people in each photo would be affected by the weather. Which element of the weather would most affect the people in each photo?

Find a map of Britain in your atlas. Locate where the people in each photo are working.

How would they be affected by the weather shown on the map opposite?

Think of other people whose jobs could be affected by the weather.

Homework

3   How accurate is the weather forecast? Listen to the TV or radio weather forecast. Make a note of the main points in the forecast. Compare the forecast with the weather the following day in your own area. How much of the forecast was correct? Did they get anything wrong?

4.2 Weather check

You don't need to have computers and satellites to forecast the weather – although they certainly help! The most important thing is to be able to observe the weather around you, and to record what you find. Most weather observation is carried out at **weather stations**. A weather station is a collection of instruments which are kept in an open area, away from buildings and trees. Your school might be lucky enough to have its own weather station.

Stevenson Screen
A box made from wooden slats, which stands on legs above the ground. The slats allow air to circulate around the box without direct sunlight reaching the instruments, which are kept inside.

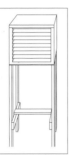

Maximum/minimum thermometer
A U-shaped thermometer with two scales to record the highest and lowest temperature each day. Columns of liquid inside the thermometer push two small pins up the tube as temperature changes. At the end of each day the pins are reset.

Rain gauge
A cylinder set into the ground to catch the rain as it falls. The rainwater is funnelled into a measuring container. The level of the water is read each day before the container is emptied.

Wind sock
A large nylon sock mounted on a pole. Wind blows into the sock and turns it in the direction of the wind. The pointer then shows where the wind is blowing from.

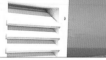

Anemometer
Three metal cups mounted on a high pole. As the wind blows it makes the cups spin. The wind speed is shown on a dial below, rather like a car speedometer.

Barometer
Mercury inside the barometer changes level as air pressure goes up or down. The higher the pressure the greater the weight of mercury it can support. The dial on the barometer reads the air pressure.

Mirror
A mirror, divided into squares, is placed on the ground where it can reflect the sky. The number of squares covered by clouds shows what proportion of the sky has cloud cover.

Freezing Below 0°C   Cold 0–15°C

Warm 15–30°C   Hot Over 30°C
Temperature

Dry   Light rain 0–2mm/hr

Moderate rain 2–10mm/hr   Heavy rain Over 10mm/hr
Rainfall

Clear sky	1/8 cloud cover	2/8 cloud cover
3/8 cloud cover	4/8 cloud cover	5/8 cloud cover
6/8 cloud cover	7/8 cloud cover	8/8 overcast

Cloud cover

Calm 0–3km/hr   Light breeze 4–15km/hr   Moderate breeze 16–35km/hr   Strong breeze 36–56km/hr   Gale 57–90km/h   Storm 91–120km/hr

Wind speed (Beaufort Scale)

Activities

1 Study the information about a weather station on the opposite page. List the instruments, and what each one is used to measure.

2 On a day in April the instruments at a weather station showed the measurements that you can see in the box below.

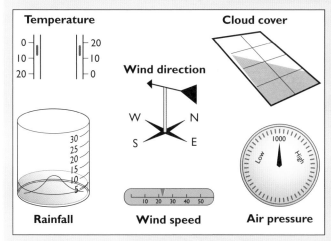

Write down each of the measurements. What words could you use to describe the weather that day? Think of words to describe the weather in your local area today.

Homework

3 Observe and record the weather in your area for a week. Do this at the same time each day at your school weather station. If you don't have a weather station, use newspaper weather reports and the words on this page to record the weather each day.

Record your observations in a table like this. Draw graphs to show temperature and rainfall. Use a line graph to record temperature and a bar graph to record rainfall.

	Mon	Tues	Wed	Thur	Fri	Sat	Sun
Date							
Temperature (°C)	x x						
Rainfall (mm)							
Wind (direction)	W						
Wind speed (km/hr)	22						
Cloud cover (⅛'s)	4/8						
Air pressure (mb)	1,000						

FRAMEWORK

4.3 The water cycle

A Steam rising from rainforest after a storm

B Ice melting to form a river

We are surrounded by water – in the sea, in rivers and lakes, underground, in living things and in the air. This water is constantly moving from one **water store** to another. As it moves, it may change from liquid water into a solid (snow or ice) or a vapour, or back again. This is called **water transfer**. Despite the many water stores and transfers, the total amount of water on the Earth stays the same. How it moves and changes is called the **water cycle**.

By far the greatest volume of water is stored in the oceans – about 97 per cent of all the world's water. The rest is fresh water, and most of this is stored in glaciers and the polar ice caps. Only 0.35 per cent of the world's water is found in the atmosphere at any one time, mostly in the form of **water vapour** (which is an invisible gas). It is this water that is responsible for giving us many different types of weather: clouds, rain, snow, hail and fog.

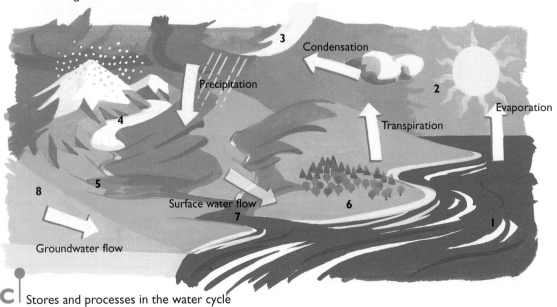

Condensation

Precipitation

3

2

Evaporation

4

Transpiration

5

8

Surface water flow

7

6

1

Groundwater flow

C Stores and processes in the water cycle

Activities

1 Look at diagram C, which shows the water cycle. Match each of the numbers with one of the places, listed in the box below, where water is stored.

> clouds groundwater ocean vegetation lake
> glacier river atmosphere

Draw your own diagram of the water cycle. Label each place where water is stored on your diagram, using one of the labels from the box in place of the numbers.

In each place add a label to say whether the water is stored as a liquid, a solid (ice) or as water vapour.

2 The arrows on the diagram show six ways in which water is transferred in the water cycle. Match each arrow with one of the descriptions in the box below.

> 1   Water from the ocean and from the land surface turns into vapour when heated by the sun
> 2   Water, in the form of water vapour, goes from vegetation into the atmosphere
> 3   Water vapour rises and cools, turning back into water droplets, which form clouds
> 4   Water droplets in clouds may get larger until they fall back to the Earth as rain, snow, hail or sleet
> 5   Water runs off the surface of the land and flows back to the ocean in rivers
> 6   Water sinks through the ground and flows slowly back to the ocean via rivers

You probably won't have enough space to add these descriptions to your diagram, so number the arrows correctly and write the descriptions in a key.

3 Look at photo D, which shows clouds rising from the island of Gibraltar, near the coast of Spain, early in the morning.

Draw a simple sketch to show the main features in the photo. Label your sketch to show:
a) Each place where water is stored
b) Each way that water is being transferred.

D | Clouds forming over the island of Gibraltar

Explain why the clouds have formed over the land, and not over the ocean. (*Clue:* the sun heats the land quicker than it heats the ocean.)

Homework

4 You are going to make your own water cycle.

You will need: a houseplant in its own pot, a large transparent plastic bag, string.

Water the soil in the pot. Carefully place the plastic bag over the plant and tie it with string beneath the pot. You have completely enclosed the plant, so that water can neither enter nor escape the bag. Leave the plant for one or two days (but not for longer or it will die from lack of air).

Observe what has happened. What do you notice?

Describe what you can see, and explain what has happened. Try to use some of the new words that you have learnt on these pages.

FRAMEWORK

4.4

Weather and climate in the British Isles

I DON'T REMEMBER IT BEING THIS NICE LAST SUMMER!

The day-to-day conditions that exist in the atmosphere are **weather**. **Climate** is the average pattern of weather that we experience over many years. Although the weather in the British Isles is quite unpredictable from one day to the next, climate hardly changes from year to year.

Britain has a **temperate** climate – that is, a climate with warm summers and mild winters. It is rarely very hot or very cold. The climate in Britain is also fairly wet throughout the year. However, there are differences in climate between one place and another, even within a small area like the British Isles.

1. Distance from the Equator (latitude)
Areas close to the Equator are hot because the sun is directly overhead during the day. Away from the Equator the sun is at a lower angle in the sky and gives less heat. The angle of the sun in the sky changes with the time of year. This is why summer is warmer than winter.

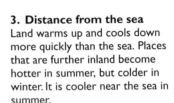

3. Distance from the sea
Land warms up and cools down more quickly than the sea. Places that are further inland become hotter in summer, but colder in winter. It is cooler near the sea in summer.

2. Height (altitude)
The higher you go in the atmosphere the colder it gets. Temperature falls 1 °C for every 150 m in height.

N

4. Wind direction
Wind often changes direction. Winds blowing from the north in the British Isles bring cold air. Winds from the south bring warmer air. The prevailing wind in Britain is from the south-west. This brings warm moist air from the Atlantic Ocean.

S

A | Reasons for differences in temperature

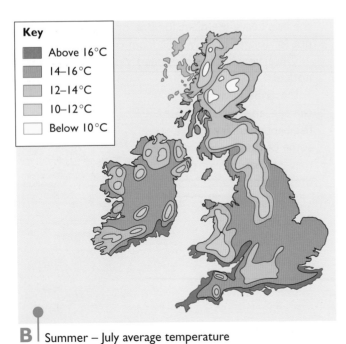

Key
- Above 16 °C
- 14–16 °C
- 12–14 °C
- 10–12 °C
- Below 10 °C

B | Summer – July average temperature

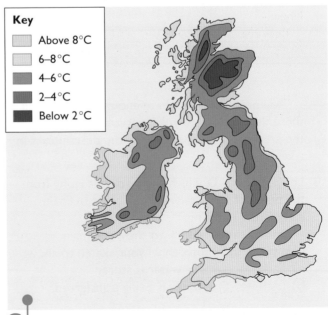

Key
- Above 8 °C
- 6–8 °C
- 4–6 °C
- 2–4 °C
- Below 2 °C

C | Winter – January average temperature

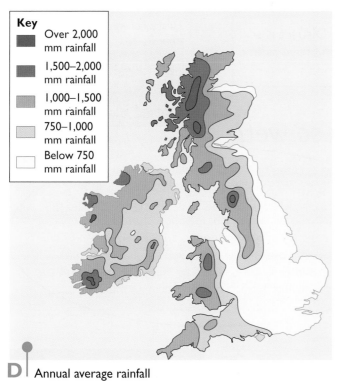

Key
- Over 2,000 mm rainfall
- 1,500–2,000 mm rainfall
- 1,000–1,500 mm rainfall
- 750–1,000 mm rainfall
- Below 750 mm rainfall

D Annual average rainfall

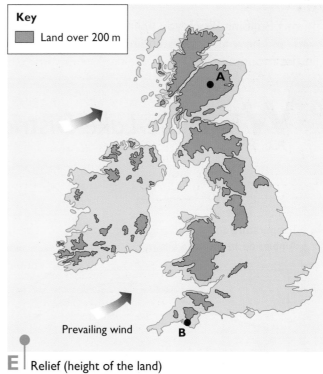

Key
- Land over 200 m

Prevailing wind

E Relief (height of the land)

Activities

1 Read the phrases in the box below. Is each one referring to the weather or the climate, do you think?

> sunny spells   average annual rainfall
> thundery showers   overnight frost
> hot summers   an unusually wet autumn

2 Look at maps B and C, which show average temperatures in the British Isles in July and January.

Re-write the sentences in the box below, choosing the correct word from each pair.

> In the British Isles it is warmer/cooler in July than in January.
> In summer the north is warmer/cooler than the south.
> In winter the north-east is milder/colder than the south-west.
> In summer and winter the lowest temperatures are found on high land/around the coast.

Explain the differences in temperature for each of the sentences you have written.

3 Look at map D, which shows the annual average rainfall in Britain. Describe the rainfall pattern in your own words.

Compare map D with map E, which shows the height of the land. Describe the link that you can see. How do you explain this?

F Winter in the Scottish mountains

4 Look at photos F and G. Locate these places on map E. Describe the weather that you can see in each photo. Is it typical at this time of year, do you think? Give reasons for your answers.

G Summer on a beach in Devon

BUILDING BLOCKS

4.5

Why is the Lake District so wet?

In this Building Block you will find out why the Lake District is so wet, and how an understanding of the weather can improve safety in the mountains.

Hilary Fouweather

I live in one of the wettest parts of the British Isles, in the Lake District. In an average year it rains here for 200 days out of 365, and the annual rainfall is over three times that of London. But there are plenty of good reasons to live here, despite the weather. It's one of the most beautiful areas I know. People come in their thousands to enjoy the lakes and the mountains here. If it didn't rain so much it wouldn't look so green!

A | Temperature and rainfall graphs for Ambleside, in the Lake District

°C
15
10
5
0

J F M A M J J A S O N D

mm
200
150
100
50
0

J F M A M J J A S O N D

Lake District

B | Walkers in the Lake District

Key

Wind direction

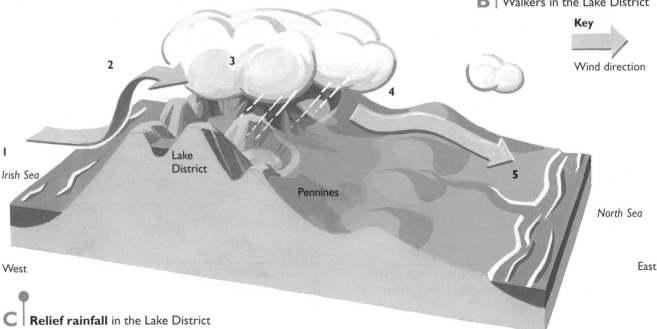

2
3
4

1

Irish Sea

Lake District

Pennines

5

North Sea

West

East

C | **Relief rainfall** in the Lake District

Activities

1 Look at diagram A, which shows temperature and rainfall graphs for Ambleside, in the Lake District.

   What is the average July temperature? What is the average January temperature? Work out the annual average rainfall.

2 Look at the table below, which shows the monthly average temperature and rainfall in London.

	J	F	M	A	M	J	J	A	S	O	N	D
Temperature (°C)	4	5	7	10	13	16	18	17	15	11	8	6
Rainfall (mm)	54	40	37	37	46	45	57	59	49	57	64	48

   Draw temperature and rainfall graphs for London.
   Compare the temperature and rainfall in London and the Lake District. What are the similarities? What are the differences?

3 Look at diagram C. Match each of the labels in the box below with one of the numbers on the diagram.

> Air warms as it descends and clouds turn back into water vapour.
> Warm air evaporates water from the sea.
> Low land to the east of the mountains receives little rain. This is a **rain shadow**.
> Clouds continue to cool over mountains and rain falls.
> Air rises and cools as it blows over the land, to form clouds.

   Write the sentences in the correct order to describe how relief rainfall happens.

4 With the help of diagram C, explain:
   a) Why this type of rainfall is called relief rain
   b) What is meant by the term 'rain shadow'.
   Look again at the rainfall map and relief map on page 73. Give two reasons explaining why the west side of the British Isles has more rainfall.

Homework

5 The sun always sets in the west. A red sky indicates that the air is dry. Try to explain why the saying 'Red sky at night – shepherd's delight' is often a reliable prediction of good weather.

   Find out some other common sayings about the weather. Try to work out whether or not they are good weather predictors.

D A sunset in the Lake District

Over the centuries people have learnt to predict the weather by looking at the sky. People who spend much time outdoors, like farmers or sailors, often have a good idea of what the weather will be like. One of the oldest sayings about the weather, 'Red sky at night – shepherd's delight', often proves to be correct.

Nowadays most people rely on the weather forecast, rather than looking at the sky. Hilary is a volunteer with the mountain rescue service in the Lake District. She is often called out to help people in trouble on the mountains when the weather suddenly gets worse. To reduce the danger, weather warnings are given for people thinking of climbing.

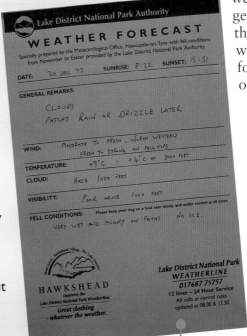

E A weather warning in Ambleside

Will it be safe on the mountain?

Unfortunately, you can't rely on weather sayings when it comes to people's safety. We need to have good, accurate weather forecasts. The Meteorological Office forecasts are usually correct. If they forecast rain and low cloud levels, we issue weather warnings to people who might want to walk or climb on the mountains. As in other parts of the country, there are weather stations in the Lake District that keep daily records of the weather and help to provide accurate forecasts.

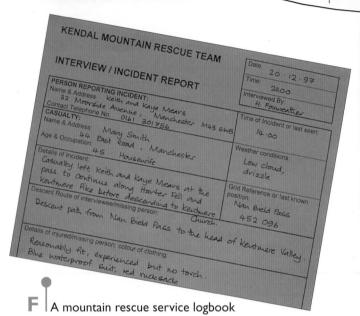

F A mountain rescue service logbook

G A mountain rescue in the Lake District

Date	Average °C Temperature	Rainfall (mm)	Wind direction	Air (mb) pressure	Date	Average °C Temperature	Rainfall (mm)	Wind direction	Air (mb) pressure
1	6.4	6.6	SW	1011	17	8.7	9.3	SE	1026
2	6.4	0.0	W	1006	18	8.5	11.5	NW	1008
3	4.6	0.0	NW	1029	19	9.0	0.6	NW	1013
4	1.9	0.8	S	1028	20	4.5	0.3	NW	1018
5	5.7	12.6	SE	1018	21	4.0	0.0	-	1025
6	2.6	1.2	-	1033	22	5.5	15.5	E	1023
7	4.8	1.6	SE	1022	23	9.0	4.7	NW	1006
8	5.0	0.0	-	1038	24	8.2	2.0	-	1007
9	4.7	4.4	-	1036	25	6.8	13.1	W	1013
10	6.2	0.0	SW	1031	26	9.0	1.8	SW	1002
11	8.8	1.5	-	1034	27	8.4	18.9	W	1013
12	5.4	1.5	-	1025	28	7.0	0.5	W	1021
13	6.7	7.5	S	1025	29	7.4	0.0	W	1026
14	8.8	4.5	W	1017	30	5.3	0.0	W	1026
15	9.2	3.9	NW	1020	31	7.7	0.0	W	1023
16	8.9	5.9	W	1023					

H Meteorological Office records from Grizedale weather station, in the Lake District, March 1997

Activities

1 Interpret map I to find out the wind direction in the Lake District on 18 March. Compare the wind on the map with the data for the same day shown in table H. Did you interpret the map correctly? Can you find out what the wind direction was like in your own area on that day?

 These activities could be done on a computer, with the help of a database and graph-drawing package. This will probably make them quicker to do.

2 Draw graphs or diagrams for each of these weather elements for March 1997 in the Lake District, using the data from H on the opposite page: a) average temperature, b) rainfall, c) wind direction, d) air pressure.

Choose a suitable style of graph to show each one.

3 Draw a scatter graph, like the ones below, to show any link between rainfall and temperature. Plot a point for each of the dates in table H.

Look at the pattern of points you have plotted. Do the points form a line? If they do, then there is a link between rainfall and temperature.

- A line sloping upwards shows a positive link – as rainfall goes up so does temperature.
- A line sloping downwards shows a negative link – as rainfall goes up so temperature goes down.

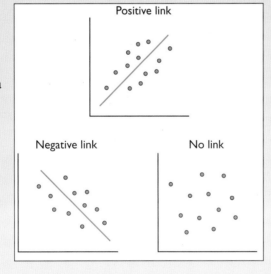

- If the points are scattered over the graph, there is no link between rainfall and temperature.

If you can see a link, draw a line onto the graph. There should be roughly the same number of points on either side of the line.

4 Draw another graph to show any link between rainfall and air pressure.

Think of how to see if there is a link between rainfall and wind direction.

5 Write three sentences describing the relationships between rainfall and temperature, rainfall and air pressure, and rainfall and wind direction.

Explain how this information could be used by the mountain rescue service. On which days in March 1997 should they have put out a weather warning for mountain climbers?

Map I shows the weather over the British Isles on 18 March 1997. The lines on the map are **isobars**. They join places with the same **air pressure**. The map shows a centre of low pressure close to the British Isles. Winds blow anti-clockwise around areas of low pressure. The closer together the isobars are, the stronger the wind blows.

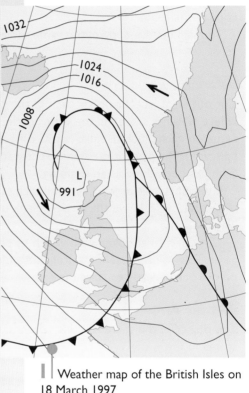

Weather map of the British Isles on 18 March 1997

Assignment

Keep a record of the weather over a few weeks. Draw graphs to present your data. Find any links between different elements of the weather. What happens when temperature rises? What happens when it falls? What happens when air pressure rises? What happens when it falls? Which wind direction usually brings rain?

In this Building Block you will play a game to find out how water moves around the water cycle.

4.6

How does the water cycle work?

Activity

Play the Water Cycle Game on the opposite page. You could play the game by yourself, or in a small group. If you play in a group, each player will need a copy of the game.

You will need: a copy of the game, a dice, scissors, card.

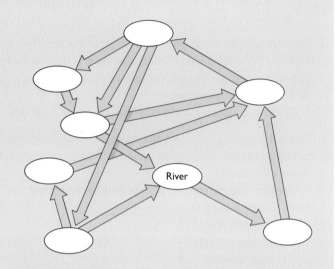

River

Before the game

Cut out eight labels, one for each of the places where water is stored in the water cycle. Write a name on each label (use diagram C on page 70 to help you), and place it on the correct water store. One has been done as an example.

Cut out twelve arrows, one for each transfer in the water cycle. Leave the arrows blank until you play the game.

Cut out a small token with which to play the game. This will represent a water molecule. Place it on the ocean ready to start the game.

Play the game

The object of the game is to visit each of the water stores in the water cycle and to complete the labels on each of the arrows.

Start the game. Each player takes a turn to roll the dice. The number on each arrow on the game shows what number you must roll to move in that direction. For example, you must roll a one to get out of the ocean. If you don't roll the number you need, you must wait until your next turn to try again.

As you move your molecule, describe how the water transfers from one store to the next. For example, as you move from the ocean you would say, 'Water evaporates from the ocean into the air.' Write the description onto an arrow. Place it on the correct arrow on the gameboard.

The game is finished when each player has visited all the water stores at least once. Each arrow should be labelled and placed on the game to show that you have been all around the water cycle.

After the game

Write an account of what happened to your water molecule during the Water Cycle Game. Name all the water stores that it visited. Describe how water transferred from one store to the next. You could start like this:

> *The water molecule began in the ocean. This is where most of the world's water is stored. It spent a long time in the ocean before it evaporated into the air. In the air, it was in the form of water vapour. Next . . .*

Assignment

Think of more water stores and transfers that you could add to the game to make it more realistic.

The average water molecule spends only about ten days in the air before it returns to the surface. Most water molecules spend thousands of years in the ocean. In what ways do you think the Water Cycle Game is like the real water cycle? In what ways is it too simple?

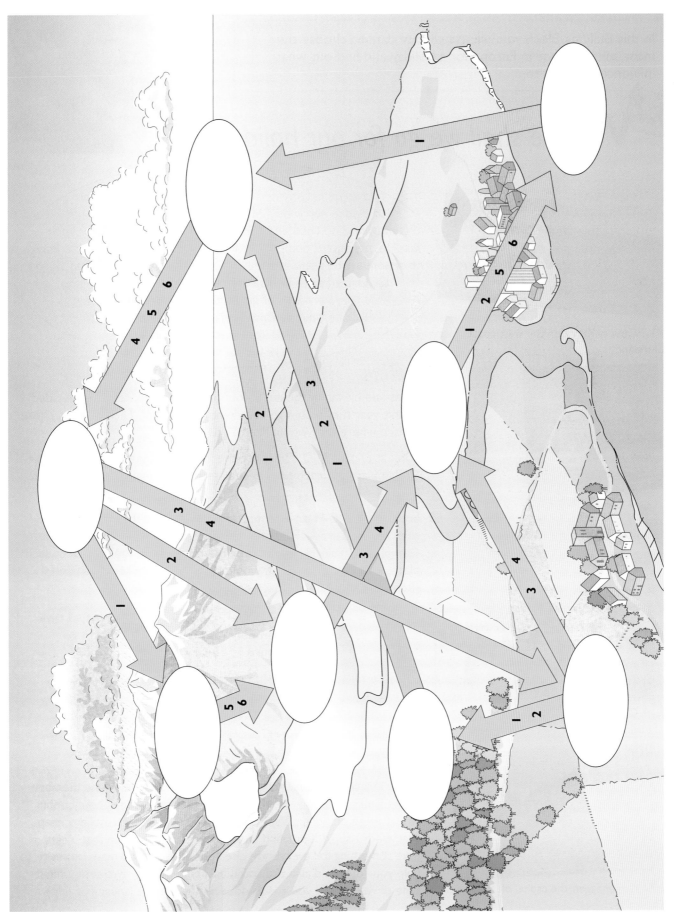

BUILDING BLOCKS

In this Building Block you will use climate data to choose the most suitable place in Europe for a holiday, and find out what influences its climate.

Thomas

4.7 **W**here shall we go for our holiday?

Our family is choosing where to go on holiday next year. As usual, it's impossible to please everybody. Mum wants to go somewhere hot and sunny, so that she can lie on a beach and read her book. Jessica, my sister, complains when it gets too hot, and gets bored on beaches. She would rather go to a place with interesting things to do. Dad says he doesn't mind where he goes, as long as there are lots of golf courses there. It could rain all the time as far as he is concerned! And me? Well, I'd like to go skiing again, like we did last year.

A County Kerry, on the west coast of Ireland

B Lech, in the Austrian Alps

C Cala Millor, on the Spanish island of Mallorca

D Copenhagen, the capital of Denmark

Activities

Thomas and his family looked at lots of travel brochures. They decided that next year they would go somewhere in Europe. Each of them chose one place where they would like to go.

1 Look at photos A–D. These are the four places that the family chose. Which place did each person choose, do you think? Use an atlas to find out where each place is.

2 Look at maps E–H on the opposite page. Locate the four places on each map of Europe. Find out what the climate in each place is like. Complete a table, like the one below, to compare the climate in each place. Decide which month would be the best time to go there. (Remember the activity each person wants to do.)

Place	Whose choice?	July temper-ature	January temper-ature	Annual rainfall	Best time to go
County Kerry					
Lech					
Cala Millor					
Copenhagen					

3 Work in a small group. Each person can take the role of one member of the family. Role play the conversation the family might have about where to go on holiday. Would any of these places for a holiday keep everybody happy? If not, find another location in Europe that might have something for everybody. Use your atlas and the maps opposite to help you. You could also use travel brochures, if you have some. What time of year would you go? (It does not have to be January or July.)

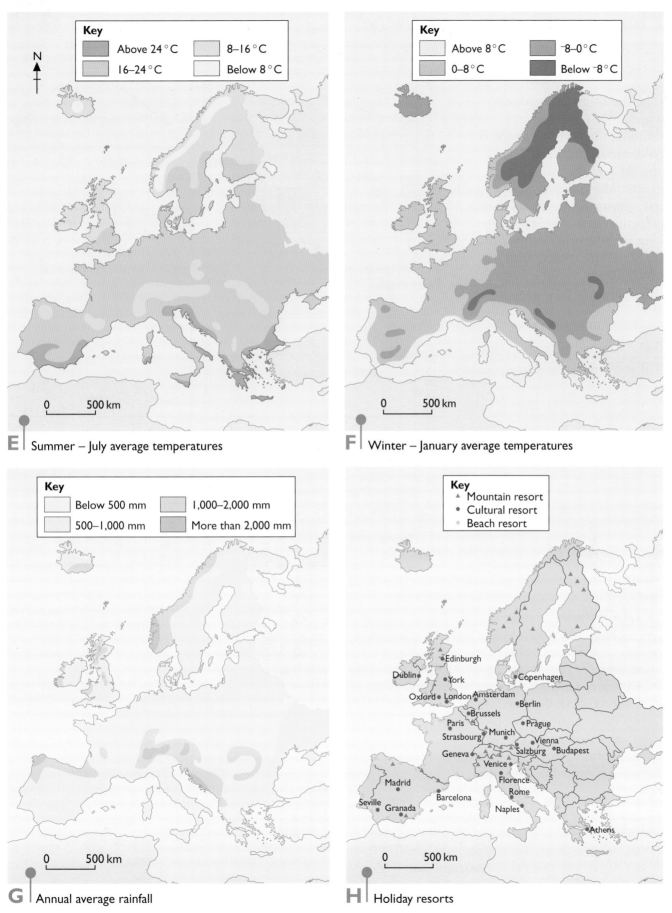

Key
- Above 24 °C
- 16–24 °C
- 8–16 °C
- Below 8 °C

0   500 km

E Summer – July average temperatures

Key
- Above 8 °C
- 0–8 °C
- ⁻8–0 °C
- Below ⁻8 °C

0   500 km

F Winter – January average temperatures

Key
- Below 500 mm
- 500–1,000 mm
- 1,000–2,000 mm
- More than 2,000 mm

0   500 km

G Annual average rainfall

Key
- ▲ Mountain resort
- ● Cultural resort
- ● Beach resort

Edinburgh
Dublin
York
Copenhagen
Oxford London Amsterdam
Berlin
Brussels
Paris Prague
Strasbourg Munich
Geneva Vienna
Salzburg Budapest
Venice
Madrid Florence
Rome
Barcelona
Seville Naples
Granada
Athens

0   500 km

H Holiday resorts

How does climate in Europe vary?

Each of the climate maps of Europe on the previous page shows some clear patterns. In July, the south of Europe is warmer than the north. In January, the east of Europe is colder than the west. The annual average rainfall is greater along western coasts and over mountainous areas than it is further east. These patterns help us to divide Europe into separate areas, each with its own climate.

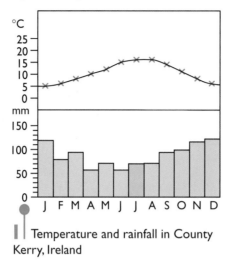

I Temperature and rainfall in County Kerry, Ireland

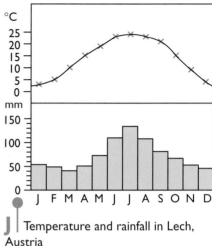

J Temperature and rainfall in Lech, Austria

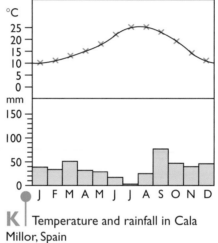

K Temperature and rainfall in Cala Millor, Spain

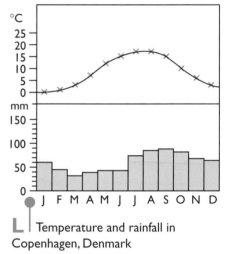

L Temperature and rainfall in Copenhagen, Denmark

Activities

1 Look at the temperature and rainfall graphs above. Choose the phrase below that best describes the climate in each place:
   a) Hot dry summers and mild wet winters
   b) Warm summers and mild winters, and wet throughout the year
   c) Warm summers and cold winters, and fairly wet throughout the year
   d) Warm summers and cold winters, but wetter in summer than winter.

2 Look again at the maps on the previous page and identify four areas in Europe, each with a different climate:
   a) Areas with summer temperature over 24 °C
   b) Areas with summer temperature over 8 °C and winter temperature over 0 °C

   c) Areas with summer temperature over 8 °C and winter temperature below 0 °C
   d) Areas with winter temperature below −8 °C.

   On your own copy of a map of Europe, draw lines to divide the continent into these four areas. Choose the best name from the box below to describe each area.

   > Mediterranean Arctic Atlantic
   > Continental European

   Mark the location of County Kerry, Lech, Cala Millor and Copenhagen onto your map. Which type of climate does each place have?

... and why?

Europe's weather and climate are controlled by different **air masses**. An air mass is a large body of air, with similar temperature and moisture content, which forms over a continent or ocean. Air masses can be continental (dry) or maritime (moist), depending on whether they formed over the land or the sea. They can also be either tropical (warm) or polar (cold), depending on whether they formed near the Equator or near the North or South Poles.

M Ice in the Arctic Ocean

Europe is a small continent, but it lies next to two large continents and the Atlantic Ocean. Air masses blow across Europe from all directions. The climate in each part of Europe tends to be controlled by one or other of these air masses at different times of year. The weather in different parts of Europe varies, as air masses compete against each other for control.

- Polar maritime air mass brings cold, moist air from the Arctic Ocean.
- Polar continental air mass brings cold, dry air from northern Asia.
- Tropical maritime air mass brings warm, moist air from the Atlantic Ocean.
- Tropical continental air mass brings warm, dry air from northern Africa.

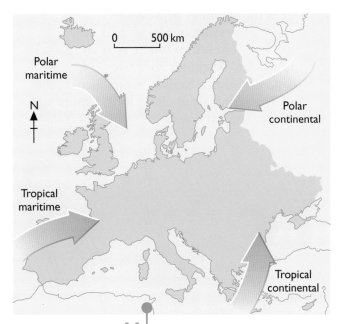

N Air masses over Europe

Activities

1 Read the newspaper headlines below. They describe some of the more extreme examples of weather in Britain. In each case, which air mass was in control of the weather, do you think? Give a reason for your answer.

| Blizzards cut off towns in Scotland |

Thunderstorms wash out tennis and cricket

Southern Britain basks in summer heatwave   It won't be a white Christmas – but it will be cold!

2 Look again at the climate graphs on the opposite page. Which air mass seems to control the climate in each place:
   a) In summer
   b) In winter?
   Draw a table like the one below. In each box write which air mass you think controls the climate. One has been started for you.

Place	Summer	Winter
County Kerry	tropical maritime	
Lech		
Cala Millor		
Copenhagen		

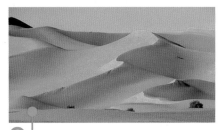

O The Sahara Desert in Africa

Assignment

Choose one of the places in Europe that you have studied. Check its location on each of the maps on page 81. Explain how each of these factors might influence its climate:
- Latitude (distance from the Equator)
- Altitude
- Distance from the sea
- Wind direction.

4.8 **W**hy is our weather so changeable?

In some parts of the world the weather is quite predictable, but that is not the case in the British Isles, where it can be warm one day and cold the next, dry in the morning and wet in the afternoon.

One of the main reasons for this changeable weather is the frequent **depressions** that affect our weather. A depression is a large area of low pressure, which develops where two air masses meet at a front. Warm air rises over colder air and, as it rises, this creates low pressure on the ground. The rising air cools to form clouds and, usually, rain soon follows.

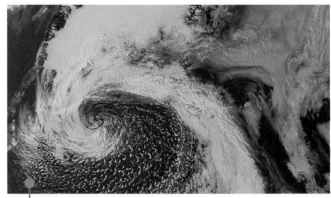

A Satellite photo of a depression

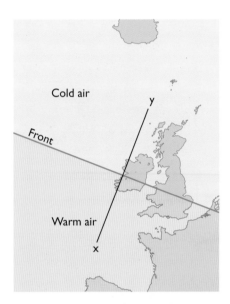

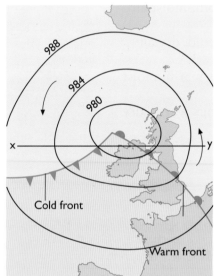

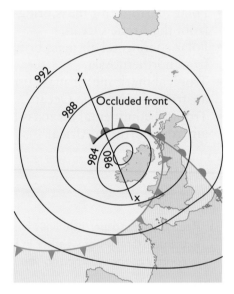

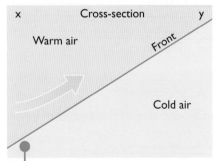

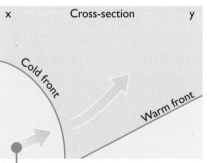

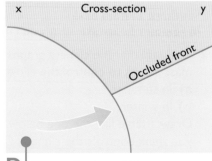

B The depressions that affect the British Isles usually form over the Atlantic Ocean. Warm air from the Equator meets cold air coming from the Arctic at a front.

C Waves develop along the front. Warm air rises over the cold air, creating a **warm front**. However, cold air is drawn in behind the warm air, in a circular motion, to create a **cold front**. It forms a spiral of cloud, typical of a depression (see in photo A). The depression is blown eastwards across the Atlantic towards the British Isles.

D Eventually, the cold front may catch the warm front ahead of it, forming an **occluded front**. The heavier cold air lifts the lighter warm air from the surface, and the depression weakens as it passes over the British Isles.

Weather forecasters use satellite photos to help them work out the path of a depression as it approaches the British Isles. From this, they can forecast what the weather will be like. The weather during the passage of a depression usually follows a similar pattern. Clouds, temperature, wind direction and air pressure each change on the ground as the depression moves across.

E Cumulus clouds often signal the passing of the depression.

F High cirrus cloud often signals the arrival of a depression.

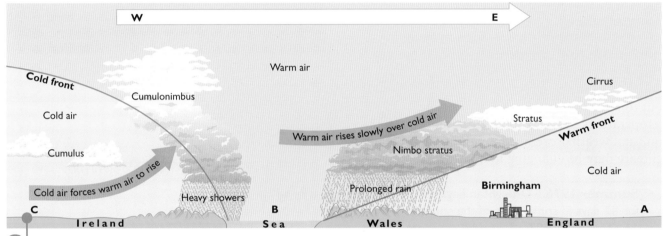

G Cross-section showing a depression across the British Isles

Activities

1 Look at diagram G, which shows a cross-section of a depression. Compare it with the weather map (right) of the British Isles. **A**, **B** and **C** on the map show the line of the cross-section. Notice the air pressure and wind direction on the map.

Choose all the correct phrases from the box below to describe the weather at points **A**, **B** and **C** on the cross-section.

> falling pressure   low pressure   rising pressure
> cold air, temperature rising   warm air
> cold air, temperature falling   southerly wind
> westerly wind   northerly wind   high cirrus cloud
> low stratus cloud   tall cumulus cloud
> approaching rain   prolonged rain
> heavy showers dying out

2 Imagine that you are a weather forecaster. Look again at the weather map. Forecast the changes in weather that people in Birmingham can expect for the next 24 hours, as the depression passes over the country.

Locate your own area on the map. How would the weather change there over the next 24 hours?

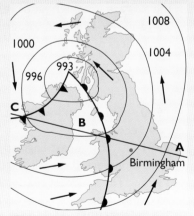

3 Observe and record changes in the weather in your own area while a depression passes over the British Isles. Listen to TV or radio weather forecasts to decide when to do this. You may need to record the weather two or three times each day. Record changes in air pressure, temperature, wind direction, cloud type and rainfall during this period. Compare your own recordings with weather maps for the British Isles during the same period. How do the maps help to explain the changes that you recorded?

DIGGING DEEPER

Is our climate changing, too?

Weather changes from day to day, but climate can also change over much longer periods of time. There is much discussion today about changing climates.

Climate change is nothing new. Until about 10,000 years ago the British Isles was in the grip of the last Ice Age, which had lasted 2,000,000 years. At the end of the Ice Age temperatures rose and the ice retreated. Since then there have been many smaller swings in temperature, including the 'Little Ice Age', which lasted from about 1550 to 1750. Temperatures were so low that the River Thames in London frequently froze. Since then, and particularly during the last century, temperatures in Britain have been rising. There is concern that this may be due not to any natural change in climate but to human activities that are causing temperatures to rise. People also point to recent unusual weather events that indicate that Britain's climate may be changing in other ways.

- **Summer 1976**   Drought in England. No rain fell for 42 days in some parts of the country.
- **16 October 1987**   Storm hit southern England. Nineteen people died in the worst storm since 1703.
- **1988–9**   The mildest winter in Britain since records began. Temperatures were 2.5 °C above the average for the time of year.
- **25 January 1990**   Another storm that affected most parts of Britain. Forty-six people killed. A month later, strong winds and high tides combined to cause coastal floods in North Wales. Hundreds of people lost their homes.
- **1990**   The second-warmest year worldwide ever recorded.
- **1991–2**   South-east England received only one-third of expected rainfall.
- **1995**   The warmest year worldwide ever recorded.
- **3 August 1995**   Highest temperature ever recorded in Britain was 37.1 °C at Chelmsford, Essex.
- **1995–7**   Prolonged drought in England. The driest 24-month period for over 100 years.
- **June 1997**   The wettest June in Britain for 140 years, but not enough to make up the water shortage from the previous two years

J Unusual weather events in Britain in recent years

H Damage from the storm that hit southern England in 1987

+ 0.4 °C

1900 1910 1920 1930 1940 1950 1960 1970 1980 1990 2000

− 0.4 °C

I Changes in global temperature during the 20th century

Activities

1 Look at graph I above. Which years had the lowest and which the highest temperatures? Describe the overall trend shown by the graph.

Homework

2 Read the unusual weather events in list J.

Do you remember any of them? Ask friends or members of your family, who do remember, to describe what happened.

Are these events good evidence of climate change, do you think? Explain your answer.

Assignment

Write a short essay entitled, 'Is our climate changing?'

Include evidence for and against the view that the British climate is changing. Do some research to find more evidence for both sides of the argument. Evaluate the arguments and write your own conclusion.

Inside a chicken production unit on a modern farm

The farm shown in the photo may be different to your image of a farm. Farming is an **industry** that has changed a lot in recent years.
- How does the photo differ from your image of a farm?
- Why do you think the hens are kept under these conditions?
- Do you think that modern farming methods like these are a good idea? Why?
- What questions would you like to ask the farmer?

GROUNDWORK

5.1 **W**here does your food come from?

Everybody used to know where their food came from. They either grew it themselves or they went to market to buy it. In some areas of the world this still happens. Today, most people in Britain buy their food in a supermarket. Most of our food is sold in packets and it comes from almost anywhere in the world. Even farmers go to the supermarket to buy their food!

As a result, few of us know much about the food we eat. What we do know is that our food still begins its journey on a farm – somewhere. Of course, it doesn't actually grow in plastic bags or cardboard boxes. That happens in factories, between the food leaving the farm and reaching your plate.

A A British supermarket

Activities

1 Look at drawing B, which shows different crops. How many would you recognise if you saw them growing on a farm?

Read the list of food products in the box below. Match each of the products with the correct crops. Some products have more than one ingredient.

> bread margarine cornflakes spaghetti
> cooking oil chocolate chips biscuits popcorn
> crisps ice-cream

2 Think of all the different foods you have eaten in the past week. Make a list.

Sort the list into two groups:
a) Food grown in this country
b) Food grown in other parts of the world. Where do you think that most of your food comes from?

Homework

3 To find out where your food comes from, look in your cupboard at home, or visit the local supermarket. Read the labels on the food, or on the packaging in which it is sold. On a map of the world, label the countries that your food comes from. Use an atlas to help you.

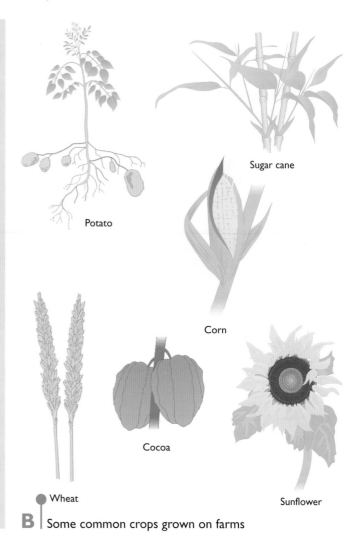

Potato

Sugar cane

Corn

Cocoa

Wheat

Sunflower

B Some common crops grown on farms

Food is vital to our health. Too little, and we become malnourished and could eventually starve. Too much food of the wrong sort, and we become overweight and prone to illness later in life. The world produces enough food for everyone to have a healthy diet. But food is not evenly shared around the world. While some countries have a **food surplus**, with more than enough to meet everybody's needs, in other countries there is a **food shortage**. Many poorer countries earn money by growing food to sell to richer countries, such as the UK. Much of the best land is taken up by these crops. As a result, local people do not have enough land on which to grow their own crops.

C A banana plantation in St Lucia, West Indies

Country	Average food intake (calories per person per day)
Australia	3,179
Bangladesh	2,019
Brazil	2,824
China	2,727
Ethiopia	1,610
France	3,633
Honduras	2,305
India	2,395
Kenya	2,075
Malaysia	2,888
Nigeria	2,124
Peru	1,882
South Africa	2,695
UK	3,317
USA	3,732

D Food consumption in different countries

The average daily calorie intake needed for a person to stay healthy is 2,400.

Remember, these are average figures. Many people in each country may get less than the average.

Activities

1 Look at photos A and C. Explain the connection between the two photos. Think of questions that you would like to ask the workers on the banana plantation. What questions might the plantation workers like to ask shoppers in a British supermarket?

2 Look at table D. Which countries have a food surplus and which have a shortage? Find the countries with the help of an atlas.

Complete a map of the world entitled, 'Food surplus and shortage'. Colour the map, using two colours to show the countries with a surplus of food and those with a shortage. Add a key. Label the countries on the map.

Compare the map with the one you labelled to show where your food comes from. Does any of your food come from countries where there is a shortage? What is the link between food shortage in some countries and surplus in others?

3 Imagine that you work for a charity, like Comic Relief, that works to educate people in Britain about world hunger. Design a poster aimed at people in Britain to explain why people in some countries are hungry.

FRAMEWORK

5.2 Natural resources

Everything we use, including the food we eat, comes originally from the natural environment. These are called **natural resources**. Wheat, fish, timber and oil are all natural resources. There may seem to be nothing natural about some of the products we use, but originally they all come from natural resources. For example, plastic is made from oil, bread is made from wheat, tables are made from wood. The way that people obtain these natural resources is called **primary industry**.

A Farming in Dorset, south-west England

B Mining in a UK colliery

Activities

1 Look at photos A–D, which show different primary industries. Which natural resources are obtained by each one?

2 Read the list of materials in the box below. Sort them into two groups – one of natural resources and one of products made from natural resources.

> glass cotton beer wheat palm oil cod plastic oil
> pine soap chair shirt water bread sand fish fingers

Match each product with the natural resource that it comes from.

3 Sort the natural resources into four groups to show which are obtained by each primary industry. Draw a table like this.

C Fishing on board a trawler

Farming	Mining	Fishing	Forestry

Think of more examples of your own to add to the table.

D Forestry in Hampshire, southern England

Industry

The word 'industry' might make you think of old factories with smoking chimneys, or a new industrial estate. In fact, industry is any type of **economic activity** – work – that people do to earn a living. Apart from primary industry, there are at least two other types of industry.

Secondary industry is the way that people make things from natural resources. It is also called **manufacturing**. This often happens in factories.

Tertiary industry is other types of work that people do. These are also known as services. Doctors, teachers, bus drivers and footballers all provide services. The main difference from other industries is that tertiary industry produces no end-product.

Activities

1 Read the list of jobs in the box below. Sort them into primary, secondary and tertiary industries.

> coal miner   pop singer   builder   baker
> fire fighter   logger   television factory worker
> fish farmer   shoemaker   bus driver   nurse
> oil rig worker   police officer   car mechanic
> shop assistant   gardener   cleaner
> nursery nurse   carpenter   accountant

2 Do a survey of people in your class to find out one job that a member of each person's family does. Sort the list into primary, secondary and tertiary jobs.

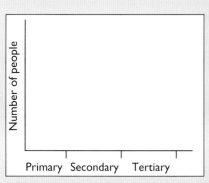

3 Draw a bar chart to show the number of people involved in primary, secondary and tertiary industry.

   What type of industry do most people in your area work in?

Homework

4 What are the main industries in your local area? If you don't know, do some research to find out. How does this help to explain the graph that you drew? Would it be the same in any part of Britain? Would it be different in other countries?

A Inside an electronics factory, an example of secondary industry

B Two examples of jobs in tertiary industry

FRAMEWORK 5.4 A mixed farm

Farming, or **agriculture**, is the way that people produce food by growing crops and raising animals. One hundred years ago, almost half of the people in Britain were farm workers. Today, only about 2 per cent of the population in Britain work on farms. They produce over half of our food. The rest comes from other countries.

Farming now produces more food from the same amount of land using fewer people.

This change has happened because each modern farm has a lot of **inputs**, such as machinery and chemical fertilizers. As a result, the farm produces a higher **output** – more crops and animals.

A Farmer using a horse-drawn plough

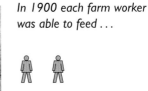

In 1900 each farm worker was able to feed . . .

B Farmer cultivating land with a tractor

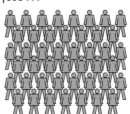

Today each farm worker is able to feed . . .

Activities

1 Read the farm diary on the opposite page. List all the words that are to do with farming. If you are not sure what any words mean, look them up in a dictionary. Write your own dictionary of farming words.

2 Make a calendar like this to show the farming year on a **mixed farm**.

Write all the jobs to do with crops on the inner circle in the correct month.

Write all the jobs to do with animals on the outer circle in the correct month.

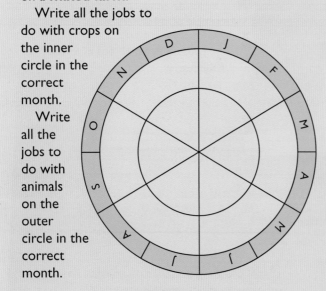

3 Draw a large diagram like the one below, to show how the farm works. Include all the processes (jobs to be done) and outputs (things produced) mentioned in the diary in the correct boxes on your diagram.

Think of all the inputs that the farm might need. These can be divided into natural inputs, such as sunlight, and those which the farmer provides, such as fertilizer. Add them to your diagram.

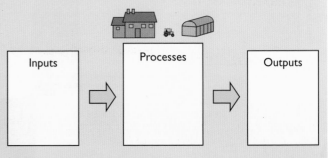

Inputs → Processes → Outputs

4 Describe what differences there might have been in the way the farm worked 100 years ago.

Penrhiw Farm is a 94-hectare farm in Wales. Like many farms in Britain, it is a mixed farm, which grows crops and raises sheep. Only two people work on the farm – Tom, who works full-time, and Eva, who works part-time. They are also the owners. These are extracts from their diary of a year on the farm.

C Tom and Eva Cowcher, the farmers at Penrhiw

January/February
Keep ewes in the fields. Feed them with hay. Bring them into the barns if there is deep snow.
Plough some fields with tractor, ready to plant spring crops.

March/April
Ewes give birth to one or two lambs each. Weak lambs get extra care indoors.
Sow spring barley and oats.

May/June
Keep ewes and lambs in the fields. They feed on grass. Shear wool from the ewes. Dip sheep in chemicals to prevent disease.
Spread fertilizer on fields with tractor to help crops and grass grow. Spray crops with herbicide to kill weeds, and pesticide to kill insects.

D Barley is the main crop. Winter barley is sown in autumn and spring barley is sown in spring. The winter barley is ready to harvest a few weeks earlier than the spring barley.

July/August
Cut grass to make hay for winter. Keep feeding lambs to make them grow fat.
Harvest barley and oats with combine harvester.

September/October
Send crops and lambs to market.
Plough some fields to sow winter barley and oats.

November/December
Mate ewes with ram, so that lambs will be born next year.
Repair machines, buildings and fences.

E The farm keeps 700 ewes (female sheep). The lambs they produce are taken to market to be sold.

FRAMEWORK

5.5 Farming in Britain

Britain has three main types of farming:

- **arable farms** – grow crops
- **livestock farms** – raise animals, usually outdoors on grass
- mixed farms – do both of these.

The farmer has to think about many physical (natural) and human factors before deciding what type of farm to be. Each of these types of farming is likely to be found in different areas. The pattern that they make on map B shows the **distribution** of farming in Britain.

- More sunshine helps crops to ripen.
- Less sunshine does not help crops to ripen.
- Warm temperatures help crops to grow.
- Cool temperatures do not help crops to grow.
- High rainfall helps grass to grow.
- Low rainfall does not help grass to grow.
- Crops need more inputs and machinery.
- Animals need fewer inputs and less machinery.
- Flat land allows machinery to be used.
- Steep land can be grazed by animals.
- Deep soil helps crops to grow.
- Thin soil allows grass to grow.
- Land is expensive close to urban markets.
- Land is cheap away from urban markets.
- High-value crops can be grown on a small area.
- Low-value grass can be grown over a large area.

A | Factors that affect farming

Activities

1 Read the list of factors that affect farming, in box A.
   Sort them into physical factors and human factors. (Physical factors are those that are natural.)

2 Look at map B, which shows the main areas of arable and livestock farming in Britain. On a large copy of the map, list, in the correct box, the factors that favour each type of farming. Put each factor under the correct heading.

3 Draw another box for the remaining area, and label it 'mixed farming'. Divide it into 'physical factors' and 'human factors'.
   Think of factors that might favour mixed farming, for example moderate temperature allows crops and grass to grow. Write these factors in the box under the correct heading.

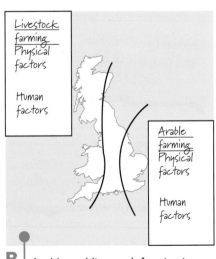

Livestock farming
Physical factors

Human factors

Arable farming
Physical factors

Human factors

B | Arable and livestock farming in Britain

Changes in the farm landscape

Farming has shaped the landscape in Britain for hundreds of years. But today the landscape is changing. In lowland areas, in the south and east, farmland is under pressure from urban growth. The total area of farmland here is shrinking. Farmers have to produce more food to feed a growing urban population on a smaller area of land. To achieve this they use more artificial inputs, like machinery and fertilizer. This is **intensive farming**. In this area, mixed farms are being replaced by farms specialising in one type of production.

In upland areas, in the north and west, there have been fewer changes in farming. Livestock farms still cover large areas. Farming here is more traditional, employs fewer people, and makes less use of machinery and other inputs. This is **extensive farming**.

C | A hill farm in North Yorkshire

D | A market garden in southern England

Activities

I Draw and label sketches of the two farms shown in the photos. Choose the correct labels from the box below.

> large fields   small fields   fewer machines   more machines
> steep land   flat land   stone walls   no walls or hedges
> grass grows with little use of chemicals
> vegetable crops grow well with use of chemicals
> sheep graze outdoors all year round
> greenhouses help crops to grow all year round

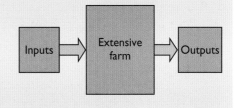

2 Draw two diagrams, like the ones here, to show how an extensive farm and an intensive farm work. Think about the inputs and outputs on each farm and list them in the correct boxes.
   Use your own words to explain the differences between extensive and intensive farming. Use the diagrams to help you.

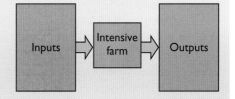

In this Building Block you will find out what decisions a farmer has to make, and try to make your own decisions.

5.6 How does the farmer decide what to produce?

We have to decide what to grow on our farm. This can depend on many factors, some physical and some human. Land around here is quite hilly and in some places the soil is poor. We get a lot of rain, especially when the wind blows from the west. Summer is not very hot, but it doesn't get very cold here either, even in winter.

Our farm is quite large so, even though the soil and climate are not perfect, we can produce a lot of crops and animals. Fortunately, the land in this part of Wales is quite cheap, but we still have to pay back the money we borrowed from the bank. It is also a long way to any large urban market so we don't grow crops that go off quickly. We produce both crops and sheep, so that we can always make some money, even when prices change.

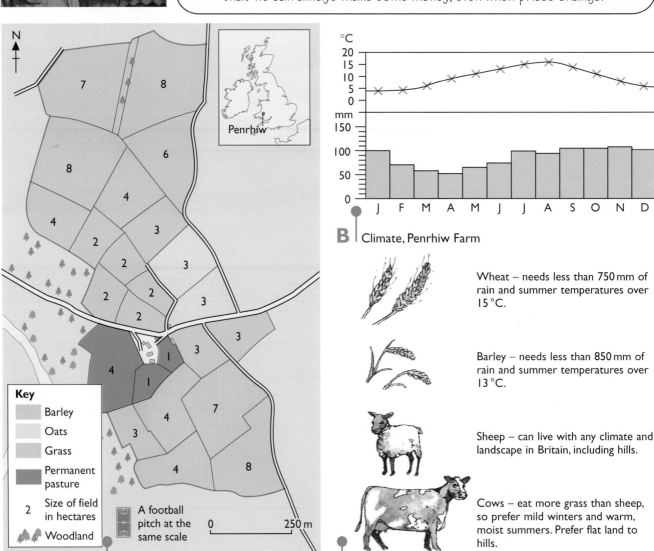

B Climate, Penrhiw Farm

Wheat – needs less than 750 mm of rain and summer temperatures over 15 °C.

Barley – needs less than 850 mm of rain and summer temperatures over 13 °C.

Sheep – can live with any climate and landscape in Britain, including hills.

Cows – eat more grass than sheep, so prefer mild winters and warm, moist summers. Prefer flat land to hills.

Key
- Barley
- Oats
- Grass
- Permanent pasture
- 2 Size of field in hectares
- Woodland

A football pitch at the same scale

0   250 m

A Penrhiw Farm

C Crops and animals

Running a farm is like running any other industry. We have to make sure that we earn more money than we spend – that's called making a **profit**. If we didn't, we would soon go out of business and have to sell the farm. This happens to many farmers.

D | Inputs and outputs

Barley

Input cost per hectare is £175 → Output is 5 tonnes per hectare at £100 per tonne

There are 34 hectares of barley

Sheep

Input cost per ewe is £20 → Output is 1.5 lambs per ewe at £40 per lamb

There are 700 ewes

E | Calculating farm profit (at 1997 prices)

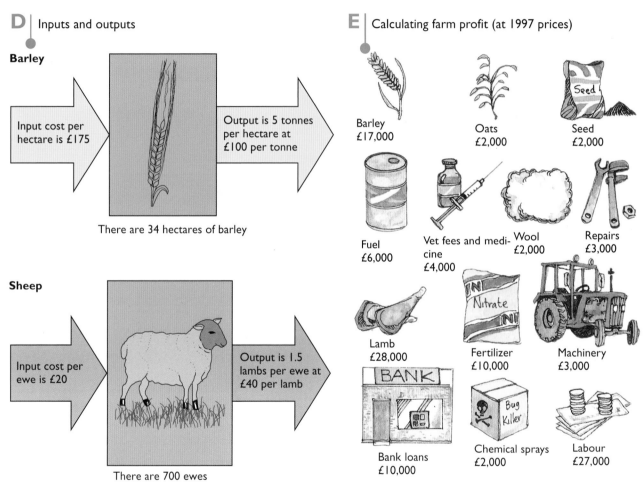

Barley £17,000

Oats £2,000

Seed £2,000

Fuel £6,000

Vet fees and medicine £4,000

Wool £2,000

Repairs £3,000

Lamb £28,000

Fertilizer £10,000

Machinery £3,000

Bank loans £10,000

Chemical sprays £2,000

Labour £27,000

Activities

1 Look at map A, which shows the size in hectares of each field.
   Work out the total size in hectares of the farm.
   Work out the area in hectares used to grow each crop.

2 Look at the information in graph B and drawing C. Explain why the farmers decided to produce barley and sheep, rather than wheat and cows.

3 Look at the information in box D. Work out which activity makes the most profit – growing barley or raising sheep. Explain why the farm continues to produce both barley and sheep, even though one is more profitable than the other. What could the farm do to increase its profit?

4 Look at drawing E. Make two lists, of the inputs and outputs on the farm, together with their value.
   Work out the annual profit that the farm makes.

   Profit = Outputs − Inputs

How should the land be used?

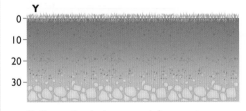

F | The landscape at Penrhiw Farm

Activities

1 Look at drawing F, which shows the shape of the land around Penrhiw Farm (Penrhiw means 'hilltop' in Welsh). The photos show the landscape at points A, B and C. Compare the drawing with map A on page 96.

2 Look at the soil profiles in drawing G. Match each profile with one of the locations on drawing F. Explain how the steepness of the land affects the depth of the soil.

3 Draw a cross-section of the farm, like the one below. Complete a table like this one to describe the three locations.

Location	Land use	Steepness	Soil depth
A			
B			
C			

Explain how the farmer might have decided how to use the land at each location.

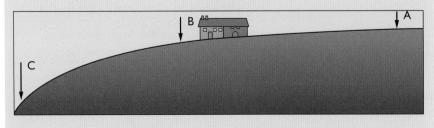

cms
X
0
10
20
30
40
50
60

Humus layer – natural organic material made from decaying plants

Soil – mixture of organic and rock fragments

Bedrock – hard rock which slowly weathers into fragments

Deep fertile soil allows plant roots to go deep. Plants grow well. Soil is easy to plough.

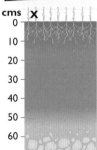

Y
0
10
20
30

Shallow soil, only deep enough for grass to grow. Without grass cover it would quickly erode.

Z
0
10
20

No soil. Tree roots grow into bedrock and produce a humus layer. Without trees bedrock would be exposed.

G | Soil on Penrhiw Farm

. . . and what about the buildings?

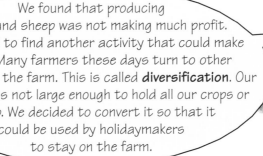

We found that producing barley and sheep was not making much profit. We needed to find another activity that could make money. Many farmers these days turn to other activities on the farm. This is called **diversification**. Our old barn was not large enough to hold all our crops or sheep. We decided to convert it so that it could be used by holidaymakers to stay on the farm.

H The old barn as it was and as it looks today

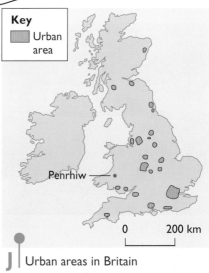

Key
Urban area

Penrhiw

0   200 km

J Urban areas in Britain

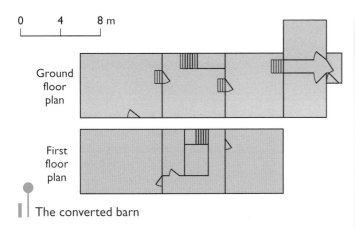

0   4   8 m

Ground floor plan

First floor plan

I The converted barn

Assignment

Design a leaflet to attract school groups to Penrhiw Farm. Include:
- Information about the accommodation
- A description of the landscape
- A map, with a farm trail to get to know the farm
- A diary of activities that happen on the farm during the year.

You can use a desktop publishing package to do this on a computer.

Activities

1 Decide which of these groups of people would be the best to attract to Penrhiw Farm. (Remember, most people are likely to come from urban areas in Britain.)
- People on day trips – usually travel less than 50 km
- People on weekend trips – usually travel less than 100 km
- People on holiday for a week or more – usually travel more than 100 km

Explain why you would try to attract this group of people. How and where would you advertise the farm to encourage these people to visit?

2 Tom and Eva decided to convert their barn to accommodate groups of up to 40 people. They expect many of these to be schools or youth groups.

Design the interior of the barn so that it could accommodate large groups. Think of the furniture you would need and how to arrange it. Draw a large-scale plan of your barn conversion.

In this Building Block you will map the distribution of types of farming in Britain, and suggest how this might change.

5.7 What types of farming can you find in Britain?

There are different types of farming in Britain. The majority of farms are still mixed farms but, today, more farms specialise in crops or livestock. The distribution of these types of farm depends on physical and human factors.

B Mixed farms produce crops and livestock. They need fairly good soil and a climate which is neither too dry nor too wet.

A Arable farms grow crops, particularly cereal crops like wheat and barley. They need flat land with deep soil and a warm, dry climate.

C Hill farms raise mainly sheep. The land is too steep to grow crops or raise cattle. Sheep can survive on any landscape or in any climate in Britain.

D **Dairy farms** raise cows to produce milk and dairy products. Other livestock farms raise cattle for beef. They need land that is not too steep and a moist climate for grass to grow well.

E Market gardens grow fruit and vegetable crops. They usually need good soil and a warm climate. Many market gardens are near to urban markets so that the fruit and vegetables will be fresh.

F **Crofts** are small-scale farms, which produce a few crops or livestock. They are found on islands and in remote areas of Scotland.

... and how is it distributed?

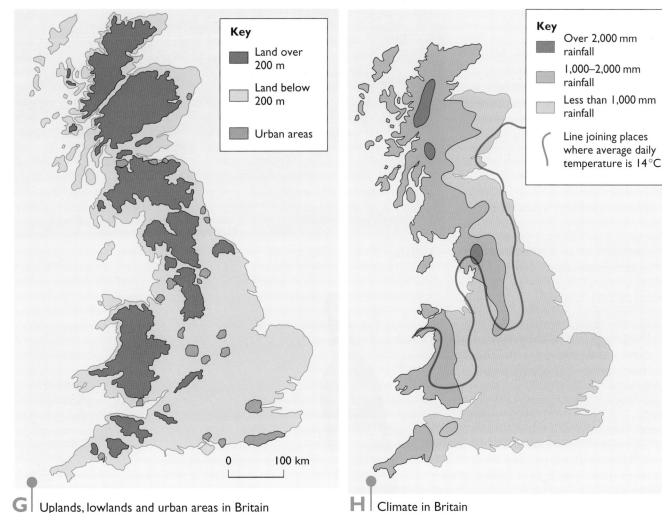

G Uplands, lowlands and urban areas in Britain

H Climate in Britain

Activities

1 Look at the location of six farms (1–6) on the map of Britain on the opposite page. Compare the location of each farm with maps G and H. For each location, find out: the height, distance from a city, rainfall, summer temperature.

2 Look at photos A–F. Match each farm with the correct location on the map. Find each location on an atlas map of Britain. What region is each location in?

3 Complete a table like the one below, describing the location of six types of farm.

4 On a map of Britain (from your teacher), draw lines to divide it into areas where you would expect to find each type of farming. Keep the map as simple as you can. Shade each area a different colour. Give your map a title.

   Compare your map with a map showing the distribution of farming in Britain. How similar are they? Explain the distribution of each type of farming.

Location	Farm type	Height	Distance from city	Rainfall	Summer temperature	Region

How is the distribution changing?

As the factors that affect farming change, so do the crops and livestock that farmers produce. Twenty years ago it was unusual to find grapes being grown in Britain. Now there are more than 400 vineyards around the country, and the number is growing.

There are many reasons for this:

A vineyard in Kent

- The climate in Britain is getting warmer, which makes it easier to grow grapes.
- New varieties of grapes have been produced, which can do well even in a cooler climate.
- People in Britain like wine and there is a growing demand for it. There is now a much larger choice of wines in shops in Britain, including some from this country.
- Farmers have found that there is reduced demand for some of their other products, so they have turned to grapes, which may make more profit.
- Many farms produce their own wine from the grapes that they grow. So they produce the raw material and manufacture it. This is another way for farms to diversify and make greater profit.

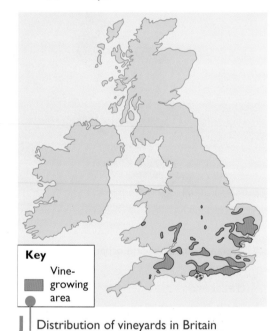

Key

Vine-growing area

J Distribution of vineyards in Britain

Activities

1 List the reasons for the growth in the number of vineyards in Britain in recent years. Which of these are physical factors and which are human?

2 Look at map J. Describe the distribution of vineyards in Britain. Explain why they are distributed like this. (The maps on page 101 may help you.)

Assignment

Read these recent newspaper headlines. Think about how each of these changes could affect the distribution of farming in Britain.

BSE crisis hits Britain – beef sales fall

Britain is getting warmer – it'll soon be like southern France

People leave highlands and islands for big cities

New technology helps fruit and veg to keep fresh longer

More young people turn vegetarian

Write a newspaper article entitled, 'Changes in British farming'. Introduce each paragraph with one of the headlines. Explain how each change could affect the distribution of farming in Britain.

In this Building Block you will consider the arguments for and against protection of natural habitats in the countryside.

5.8 What sort of landscape do we want?

Since the Second World War, when food in Britain was rationed, the main priority for farmers has been to increase food production. Over the past 50 years or so they have successfully achieved this. The country now produces more of its own food, and imports less, than it did in 1945.

The cost of this policy has been the loss of much of the traditional farming landscape. Farmers have turned to more intensive farming methods, using more machinery, more chemical fertilizers and pesticides, and keeping more livestock indoors. Some of the natural wildlife **habitats** that were once common in the countryside have begun to disappear. Hedgerows and woodlands have been cleared, meadows have been ploughed up and wetlands have been drained.

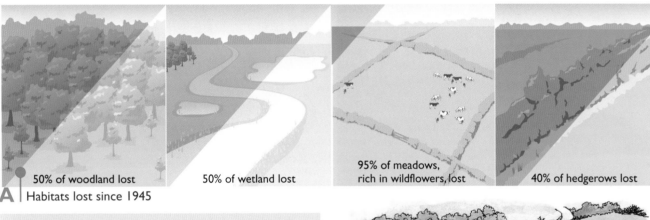

50% of woodland lost   50% of wetland lost   95% of meadows, rich in wildflowers, lost   40% of hedgerows lost

A Habitats lost since 1945

Activities

1 Look at the diagrams in A. Write four sentences about the changes in the farming landscape that they describe.

2 Look at drawing B, which shows what a typical farming landscape would have looked like 50 years ago. Draw the same area as it might look today. Use the data on this page to help you. For example, 40 per cent of the hedgerows would not be there, so fields would be larger.

   Include other changes in your drawing, such as new buildings, modern machinery, less livestock and more crops.

3 Imagine that you were to interview the farmers who had changed the landscape shown in your picture. What reasons do you think they might give for the changes?

B A typical farm landscape, 1945

Should farmers look after the landscape?

Most natural habitats in the countryside need to be managed. For example, many hedgerows were planted hundreds of years ago to act as field boundaries and stop livestock from wandering. It tends to be farmers who have to manage them. As farming methods change, it is often easier to remove them.

Conservationists are people who think that natural habitats need to be protected. Farmers and conservationists often disagree about how much protection should be given to natural habitats in the landscape.

D | A hedgerow habitat

C | A mature hedgerow

Hedges need a lot of work to keep them neat

Hedges are an obstacle to large machinery

Hedges are a habitat for wildlife

Hedges can't be moved easily, but fences can

Hedges take up space that could be used to grow crops

Hedges provide a home for some crop pests and for weeds

Hedges keep farm animals in the fields

Hedges provide shelter from wind and rain to farm animals

Hedges make the landscape look more interesting

Hedges protect the soil from strong winds and prevent soil erosion

Activities

1 Read the arguments used by farmers and conservationists for and against keeping hedges.

   List the arguments that would be:

   a) Used by the farmer in favour of removing hedges
   b) Used by the conservationist in favour of keeping hedges.

2 With a partner, role play a discussion between a farmer and a conservationist. In your roles, argue for and against removing hedges.

. . . and who should pay?

The government's priorities for the countryside have begun to change. Although it still expects farmers to produce food, it also wants them to look after the landscape. With the **European Union**, it has introduced schemes to encourage farmers to do this. The Environmentally Sensitive Areas (ESA) Scheme pays farmers to manage natural habitats in areas where they are in danger of being lost. They are paid a grant for each year that they take part in the scheme. This usually means they must farm using less intensive methods and make less profit. The Farm Woodland Scheme pays farmers to plant new woodland on arable land – particularly broadleaved trees such as oak or beech, which have been largely lost in the last 50 years. Farmers receive a grant for each hectare that they plant.

Pympes Court Farm, near Maidstone in Kent, manages many of its wildlife habitats

Activities

1 The natural habitats in photos E–I are: woodland, hedgerow, flower meadow, pond and orchard. Match each photo to a type of habitat. What wildlife would you expect to find in each of these habitats?

2 Farmers earn more money for their cereal crops than they receive as grants for managing habitats. If you were a farmer, decide whether you would want to take part in the ESA Scheme or the Farm Woodland Scheme. What factors might it depend on?

Assignment

Through our taxes, everyone pays for the grants that farmers receive.
    Prepare for a class debate on the motion, 'If we want farmers to look after the landscape, we need to pay them.' Decide whether or not you agree with this statement. It might help you to think about these questions:
- Who owns the landscape?
- How important is it to protect the landscape?
- Who should pay to protect the landscape?
- Is it fair to expect farmers both to grow food and to protect the landscape?

Write a short speech that you could make in the debate. Debate the motion with your class. Some of the class can represent farmers and the others can be taxpayers and conservationists.

DIGGING DEEPER

5.9 **N**ever mind the quantity . . .

Farmers have become victims of their own success. They have done their job so well that they produce more food than we need. In Britain, and in other European countries, there is a surplus of many basic foods. Wheat, butter, wine and milk are just some of the products that have to be stored because there is too much to eat. The amounts stored are so huge that they are sometimes called **food mountains** or **food lakes**.

Farmers have been encouraged by their own governments and by the European Union (EU) to grow such quantities. The EU pays farmers a guaranteed price, or **subsidy**, for the food they grow, whether they are able to sell it or not.

In recent years, faced by increasing surpluses, the EU has tried to find ways to persuade farmers to grow less. One way is to pay them to grow nothing at all! In a policy called '**set-aside**', farmers, growing mainly cereals, are paid £200 per hectare to leave at least 20 per cent of their land without crops. They must do this for at least five years. Usually the land is left to grow grass, although it could be used for planting trees or even for building.

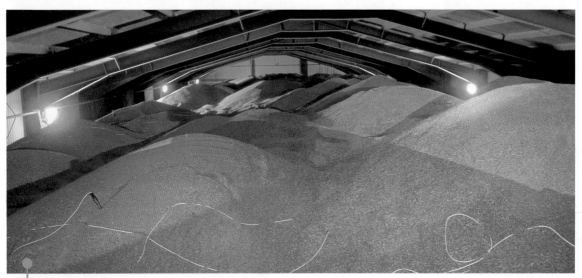

A A food mountain held by the EU

FRIENDS OF THE EARTH SAY 'SET ASIDE SET-ASIDE'

The environmental organisation Friends of the Earth has criticised the European Union policy of set-aside. It argues that it is ridiculous to pay farmers to do nothing and that it does not encourage them to put the land to good use. It suggests that, on many farms, set-aside land will just be used as a dump, or be allowed to become overgrown. And it may not solve the problem of overproduction. Farmers may choose to set aside the poorest land on their farms and continue to produce more crops on their best quality land with the help of high inputs of fertilizer and pesticides. It points out that, with over 4 million hectares of arable land in the UK, the set-aside policy could leave an area the size of Lincolnshire to grow nothing. If surpluses continue to grow in the EU, that area could become even larger.

B

Activities

1 Explain, in your own words:
   a) Why the EU has introduced the set-aside policy
   b) Why groups like Friends of the Earth think it will not work.

2 Suggest what each of the following groups of people may think about the EU policy of set-aside as a solution to the problem of food surpluses:
   a) Farmers in Europe
   b) Food consumers in Europe
   c) People living in countries where there is a food shortage.

... is it safe to eat?

People today are concerned about the quality of the food we eat and the water we drink. These are both affected by modern farming methods. Pesticides and herbicides, which farmers spray on the crops to kill insects and weeds, may also have a harmful effect on people. Farmers protect themselves when they use these chemicals. Unfortunately, chemical residues can still be found on some crops when they reach consumers.

Meanwhile, fertilizers, especially nitrates, can be harmful to health when they are washed through the soil and into our water supply. In Britain, drinking water in some areas has been found to contain unsafe levels of nitrates. High levels of nitrates in rivers also kill river life, by encouraging a few plants to grow rapidly, using up the oxygen in the water.

Water supplied to people's homes may contain pollution from farming.

Sewage from animal rearing may be washed into rivers. This too increases nitrate levels.

Pesticides sprayed onto crops may be left as a residue and may also find their way into rivers.

Fertilizers added to the soil may be washed into rivers. Nitrates kill river life and are unsafe to drink.

C | Water pollution caused by conventional farming methods

D | Organic products (left) are often smaller and of less regular shape than those produced with chemicals

Concern about conventional farming methods has led people to demand food that is safe to eat. **Organic farming** is an alternative way of producing food, which does not use artificial (inorganic) chemicals. Instead, animal manure is used to maintain soil fertility, and **crop rotation** is practised, so that the soil is given time to recover between crops.

Organic farming is often less intensive and may cause less damage to natural habitats. However, crop and animal **yields** are lower, and the crops may not look as attractive as those produced by using chemicals. Some farmers are prepared to try using organic methods. They receive higher prices for their products because consumers are willing to pay more.

Activities

1 Complete a large table like the one below, listing the advantages and disadvantages of conventional farming and organic farming methods.

	Conventional farming	**Organic farming**
Advantages		
Disadvantages		

2 Suggest what the following groups of people might think about the use of organic farming methods instead of conventional farming:
   a) Farmers in Europe
   b) Food consumers in Europe
   c) People living in countries where there is a food shortage.

DIGGING DEEPER

What are the benefits of organic farming?

... for farmers?

> If I turned to organic farming it would take three years to get all the chemicals out of the soil. In that time my yields would go down and I would get less money. Will people still want organic food when I start to produce it? I might find that I can't sell it.

Conventional farm

Total input cost is £220 → 7 tonnes of wheat at £150 per tonne

Organic farm

Total input cost is £90 → 4 tonnes of wheat at £200 per tonne

E Costs and prices of growing two types of wheat

... for consumers?

	Regular price	Organic price
Carrots	42p/kg	89p/kg
Potatoes	33p/kg	45p/kg
Tomatoes	55p/kg	£1.22/kg
Apples	£1.30/kg	£1.49/kg
Milk	28p/pint	41p/pint
Cheese	£4.89/kg	£7.59/kg
Yoghurt	19.8p/100 g	19.8p/100 g
Oats	7p/100 g	13p/100 g

F Pricecheck (at 1997 prices)

... for the environment?

> Instead of paying farmers to grow nothing, the European Union could pay them to grow organic food. By doing this, they could reduce surpluses and improve food quality at the same time. Not only that, farming would harm the environment less. If more farmers grew organic food, it would become cheaper and more people could afford to buy it.

Activities

1 Work out how much profit a farmer can make producing a field of wheat:
   a) On a conventional farm
   b) On an organic farm.
   Answer these questions:
   • Why are yields lower on an organic farm?
   • Why does the farmer receive a higher price for organic produce?
   • Which type of farm will give the greatest profit?

Homework

2 Do a consumer survey – either in pairs at your local supermarket, or among people you know.
   Find out if people know what organic food is. If not, explain it to them.
   Show them samples of organic food or the photo on page 107, to compare with other produce.
   Which do they prefer? Would they be willing to pay more for organic food? How much would they be willing to pay?

Assignment

Write a report for the European Union Commission for Agriculture, arguing either for or against more organic farming in the EU.
   Use the results of your consumer survey and the rest of the information in this unit to help you to decide which side of the argument you will take.
   Think about the needs of farmers, consumers, the environment and people in other parts of the world.

Tourist attractions in France

France is a popular destination for tourists from other countries. Sixty million people visit France every year. These are some of the places that they go to.

- Can you recognise any of the places in the photos?
- What features can you see that would attract tourists?
- What features in the photos might you find in Britain? Are there any differences?
- How typical of France do you think these photos are?

GROUNDWORK

6.1 Postcards from France

France is our closest neighbour in Europe. British people visit France more than they visit any other country, either on day trips or for longer holidays. Since the opening of the Channel Tunnel in 1994, you can travel by train from London to Paris in three hours, less time than it takes to travel from London to Newcastle.

A Routes to France

Activities

1 Think about what preparations you might have to make if you were to go to France on holiday. The pictures will give you some clues. Make a list of the preparations you would make.

2 Think of simple questions that you might need to ask when you are in France, such as: 'Where are the shops?' Find out how to ask the questions in French.

3 Look at map A, which shows transport routes in France and Britain. Match the four destinations (A, B, C, D) with the photos on the previous page. Which place would you choose to go to? Plan a route to travel there.

Homework

4 Find out more information about travel to France from a local travel agent. What would be the best means of travel to your destination? Think about the time, distance and cost of the journey.

J'adore la France – C'est très sympathique!

Activities

1 Look at photos B–E, which show different places in France. They also show the average temperature in January and July and the average rainfall.

Decide which of these activities you could do at each place.

> skiing swimming climbing
> sunbathing sightseeing
> walking canoeing shopping
> sailing theatre-going

2 Complete a table like the one below, comparing the four places. Suggest what time of year would be best to go to each place. Give a reason.

B Paris

Temperature Rainfall
25 20 S 15 10 5 W 0 | 1,000 500
S = Summer **W** = Winter

C The Alps

Temperature Rainfall
25 20 S 15 10 5 0 W | 1,000 500
S = Summer **W** = Winter

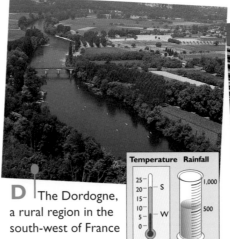

D The Dordogne, a rural region in the south-west of France

Temperature Rainfall
25 20 S 15 10 W 5 0 | 1,000 500
S = Summer **W** = Winter

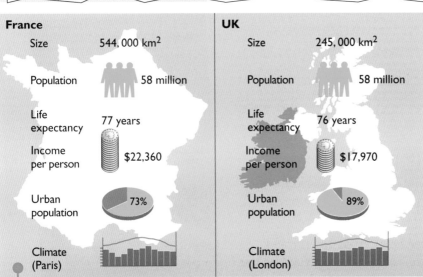

E The Mediterranean coast, south of France

Temperature Rainfall
25 S 20 15 10 5 W 0 | 1,000 500
S = Summer **W** = Winter

Letter	Place	Summer temperature	Winter temperature	Rainfall	Activities	Best time to go	Reason

France

Size	544, 000 km²
Population	58 million
Life expectancy	77 years
Income per person	$22,360
Urban population	73%
Climate (Paris)	

UK

Size	245, 000 km²
Population	58 million
Life expectancy	76 years
Income per person	$17,970
Urban population	89%
Climate (London)	

F France and the UK compared

3 Look at the data in box F, which compares France and the UK.

Describe three differences between France and the UK.

Describe three similarities between France and the UK.

4 Imagine that you are on holiday in France. Write a postcard to a friend from one of the four places. Mention how you travelled, what the weather is like, what you have done and how the place compares with where you live.

6.2

Landscape and climate in France

Landscape and climate together describe the **physical geography** of a country.

The landscape of France can be divided into three main areas – lowland areas in the north and west; upland areas, found mainly in the Massif Central; and the mountain ranges of the Alps and Pyrenees to the south. Most of the rivers start in the mountains and upland areas and flow northwards or westwards to the sea.

The Alps and Pyrenees are both **fold mountain** ranges, formed by movement in the Earth's crust, which has lifted the rock. They are the highest mountains in Europe, and Mont Blanc is the highest peak. The Massif Central is an older area of mountains which has been worn down to form a **plateau**, into which rivers have eroded deep valleys. The area was formed millions of years ago from volcanoes that are now extinct.

A Coastline in Brittany, northern France

B The Ardeche river gorge

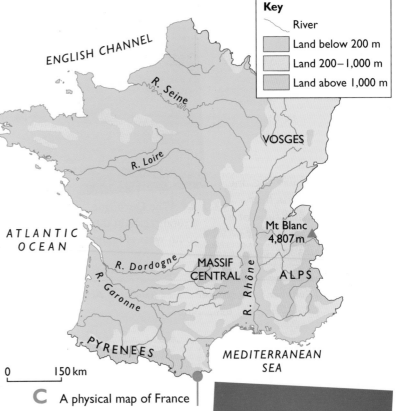

Key

River
Land below 200 m
Land 200–1,000 m
Land above 1,000 m

ENGLISH CHANNEL

R. Seine

VOSGES

R. Loire

ATLANTIC OCEAN

Mt Blanc 4,807 m

R. Dordogne

MASSIF CENTRAL

R. Rhône

ALPS

R. Garonne

PYRENEES

MEDITERRANEAN SEA

0   150 km

C A physical map of France

Activities

1 Look at photos A, B and D. What three types of erosion are at work? How could each of these places be used by people?

2 Measure the length of each of the rivers on the map, using the scale. Which is the longest river in France? How long is it?
   Find out in which mountain or upland area each river has its source, and in which direction it flows. Which river does not flow north or west?

3 On a copy of the map, mark each of the cities listed on page 114. How many of these cities are found on rivers? How many are on the coast? Suggest why they are located there.

D The Alps mountain range

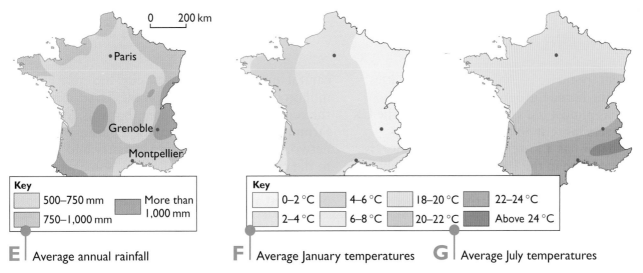

E | Average annual rainfall

Key

500–750 mm	More than 1,000 mm
750–1,000 mm	

F | Average January temperatures   G | Average July temperatures

Key

0–2 °C	4–6 °C	18–20 °C	22–24 °C
2–4 °C	6–8 °C	20–22 °C	Above 24 °C

France has a variety of climates. In summer, the warmest part of France is the south, which is closest to the Equator. In winter, the mildest part is the west, which is warmed by the ocean currents of the Atlantic Ocean. Mountain areas are colder at all times of year.

Rainfall is high in the west where moist winds blow from the Atlantic. Mountain areas have the most precipitation because air has to rise over them. As the air cools it produces rain or snow.

Activities

1 Look at maps E, F and G, which show the climate in France. Match each of the three places on the maps with the description of their climate:

• Warm summers (over 18 °C) and cool winters (2–4 °C) with less than 750 mm of rain

• Hot summers (22–24 °C) and cold winters (less than 2 °C) with more than 1,000 mm of rain

• Hot summers (22–24 °C) and mild winters (over 6 °C) with less than 750 mm of rain.

Choose the best word to describe the climate in each place: mountain, Mediterranean or temperate.

2 Look at drawing H, which shows an area of the Alps in winter. Decide where you would be most likely to find each of these activities:

• Skiing in winter and cattle grazing in summer

• Mountain climbing

• Forestry and some livestock farming

• Villages, ski resorts and mixed farming.

Draw a sketch to show the same landscape in summer. Label each of the above activities in the correct place on your sketch.

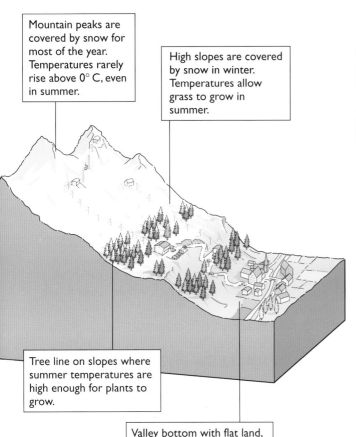

Mountain peaks are covered by snow for most of the year. Temperatures rarely rise above 0° C, even in summer.

High slopes are covered by snow in winter. Temperatures allow grass to grow in summer.

Tree line on slopes where summer temperatures are high enough for plants to grow.

Valley bottom with flat land, where temperatures only fall below freezing in midwinter.

H | A winter landscape in the Alps

6.3 People in France

Settlement, population and economic activities describe the **human geography** of a country. France has almost the same population as the UK but it covers more than twice the area. This means that it has a lower population density (is less crowded) than the UK. The most densely populated areas in France are around the major cities and industrial areas. Paris, which is the capital and by far the largest city, has over 9 million people. It grew up on the River Seine at the centre of a flat fertile area that was good for farming. It is also the centre of the transport network in France, bringing industry and people to the city. The Rhône Valley and some parts of the coast are also fairly crowded. The most thinly populated areas are the mountains and uplands.

A Population density

City	Population (in thousands)
Bordeaux	696
Grenoble	405
Lille	959
Lyons	1,262
Marseilles	1,231
Nantes	496
Nice	517
Paris	9,319
Toulon	438
Toulouse	650

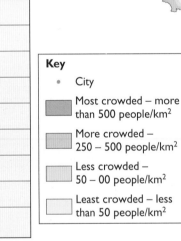

Key
- • City
- Most crowded – more than 500 people/km²
- More crowded – 250 – 500 people/km²
- Less crowded – 50 – 00 people/km²
- Least crowded – less than 50 people/km²

0 ———— 150 km

Activities

1 Look at the map, which shows population density in France.

   Describe which parts of France are:
   a) Most crowded
   b) Least crowded.
   Use directions and features on the physical map on page 112 to help you. For example, the south-west of France, around the Pyrenees, is one of the least crowded areas.

2 Read the list of factors that affect population density in the box below.

> cold climate warm climate flat land
> steep land good soil poor soil
> near to coast inland good water supply
> poor water supply good roads and railways
> poor transport industry no industry

Think about which factors are likely to make an area more crowded, and which would make it less crowded.

   List the factors in two columns.

   Compare the map with the maps of France on pages 112 and 113. Can you prove whether any of your ideas are correct?

Homework

3 List the cities of France in order of population.

   Find out the population of the ten largest cities in Britain. Compare the two lists. What differences and similarities do you notice?

6.4 Regions of France

France is divided into 22 regions, including the island of Corsica in the Mediterranean. The boundaries of each region were set by the French government to make it easier to run France and to plan change in each part of the country.

Each region differs in its landscape, climate, population and economic activities. There are also differences in the history and culture of the regions and, in some cases, even language.

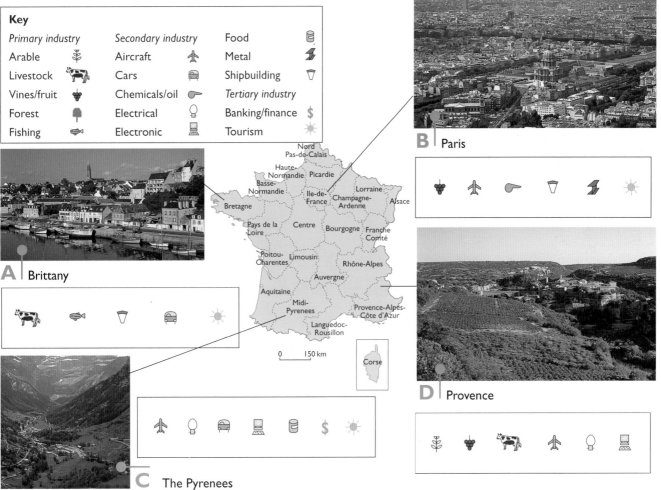

Key

Primary industry
Arable
Livestock
Vines/fruit
Forest
Fishing

Secondary industry
Aircraft
Cars
Chemicals/oil
Electrical
Electronic

Food
Metal
Shipbuilding

Tertiary industry
Banking/finance $
Tourism

B Paris

A Brittany

C The Pyrenees

D Provence

Activities

1 Work in a small group.

Choose one of the regions shown in photos A–D. Make sure that each region has been chosen.

Locate your region on each of the maps you have already looked at in this unit. Find out as much as you can about the region. Share the information with people in the group who have found out about different regions.

Complete a large table like the one below comparing the regions.

2 Study the table that you have completed. Which of these regions is most like your home region? Which is the least like it? Give reasons for your answers.

Region	Landscape	Climate	Cities	Population density	Primary industry	Secondary industry	Tertiary industry

FRAMEWORK

6.5 France in Europe

France was one of the founder members of the European Union (EU), which was created in 1957. The EU was set up to develop **trade** within Europe. It became cheaper for member countries to **import** and **export** goods to and from other member countries. It also became easier for people from member countries to travel, and to find work, anywhere in the EU.

Today, the EU has grown to fifteen member countries, with a combined population of nearly 400 million. Other countries in eastern Europe are waiting to join. The EU has increased **interdependence** between the countries of Europe. France is now part of one of the world's richest and most powerful groups of countries.

Key

☐ Joined in 1957	A	Albania	M¹	Macedonia
☐ Joined in 1973	B	Belgium	M²	Moldova
☐ Joined in 1981	B-H	Bosnia-	N	Netherlands
☐ Joined in 1986		Herzegovina	S¹	Slovenia
☐ Joined in 1995	C	Croatia	S²	Switzerland
☐ Not members	L	Luxembourg	Y	Yugoslavia

0   500 km

A The European Union

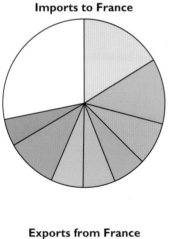

Imports to France

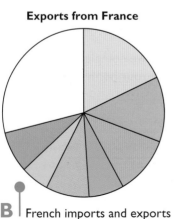

Exports from France

Key

☐ Germany
☐ Italy
☐ Belgium
☐ UK
☐ Spain
☐ Netherlands
☐ USA
☐ Japan
☐ Others

B French imports and exports

C Farmers in the European Union receive guaranteed prices for their products. Some farms, like this vineyard in the south of France, also receive money to modernise.

The European Union budget had grown to about £60 billion by 1996. This sounds like a huge amount of money, but only amounts to about 1 per cent of the income of all the EU countries. Each country in the EU contributes money according to its wealth, with the richest countries paying more. The poorer countries receive most help from the EU. Table D shows the proportion of the EU budget contributed and received by each country in 1996.

Plans have been made to strengthen the EU by moving towards even greater union between the member countries. As a result of the **Maastricht Treaty** in 1993, citizens of member countries are also citizens of the EU, laws concerning living and working conditions are the same throughout the EU, and there will even be a European police force.

Perhaps the most important outcome of the Treaty will be monetary union. This means that, instead of each country having its own currency, they all use European money called the 'Euro'. France, as one of the most important countries in Europe, is at the heart of these changes. However, many people are worried that national governments will lose their power and the EU will become the 'United States of Europe'.

D | Contributions and receipts from the EU budget in 1996

Country	Contribution (% EU budget)	Receipt (% EU budget)	Gain or loss
Germany	29.1	14.4	Loss
France	17.7	8.9	
Italy	11.6	14.5	Gain
Netherlands	5.7	1.5	
Belgium	3.7	1.3	
Luxembourg	0.2	0.1	
UK	12.6	7.2	
Ireland	1.1	4.2	
Denmark	1.8	0.5	
Greece	1.4	10.5	
Spain	6.3	22.9	
Portugal	1.5	10.8	
Austria	2.7	1.1	
Finland	1.4	1.2	
Sweden	2.5	1.0	

I'm glad that France is part of the EU. We are able to do more trade and that makes us better off.

We have to give too much money to Europe. Now they want to make our laws too. Vive la France!

Activities

1 Look at map A. Which countries were the founder members of the EU? When did the UK join?

2 On a copy of the pie charts, shade the parts that show trade with other EU countries. What percentage of France's trade is with EU countries?

3 On a copy of table D, work out which countries gain and which lose from being an EU member.
   Colour a map of Europe in two colours to show:
   a) Countries that gain money in the EU
   b) Countries that lose money in the EU.
   What pattern do you notice about the location of the countries on the map that you have coloured?

4 Imagine that you live in France. List all the arguments that you can find on these two pages for and against being a part of the EU.

Homework

5 Carry out an opinion poll of people you know, or, in pairs, in your local area. Find out whether or not people in Britain want to be a part of the EU. Would you expect people in France to have similar ideas? Give reasons for your answer.

In this Building Block you will find out what Ile-de-France is like, and choose the area there where you would prefer to live.

6.6 Why go to Ile-de-France?

I'm going to Ile-de-France with our school. When the teacher told us, none of us knew where it was. Then she explained that Ile-de-France is the region around Paris. Everybody knew something about Paris: it's a big city a bit like London, the Eiffel Tower is there, it has a Métro, and there are lots of shops and cafés. Apart from that, Disneyland, Paris is just nearby. We all got very excited. Some of us have pen pals in Paris and we hope to meet them, too.

Davinder

A Central Paris street plan

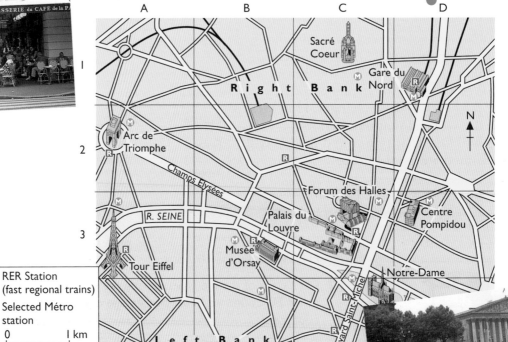

R RER Station (fast regional trains)

M Selected Métro station

0   1 km

Activities

1 Look at map A. Find each of the tourist attractions listed below. Give the square on the map where you would find each place, for example, the Tour Eiffel is in A3.

> Tour Eiffel   Arc de Triomphe   Palais du Louvre
> Musée d'Orsay   Sacré Coeur
> Centre Pompidou   Notre-Dame   Forum des Halles

2 Choose the places that you would most like to visit if you were spending a weekend in central Paris. Plan a route around Paris to visit them. Start and finish at the Gare du Nord, where the Eurostar train from London arrives.

For each part of the route, decide whether you would walk or take the Métro, and give directions and distances. Draw a sketch map to show your route.

The trip that everyone is looking forward to is Disneyland, Paris. It's about 30 km east of Paris, near the town of Marne-la-Vallée. We can get there on a high-speed RER train. Disney is an American company, not a French one. I wonder why it decided to come to the Ile-de-France?

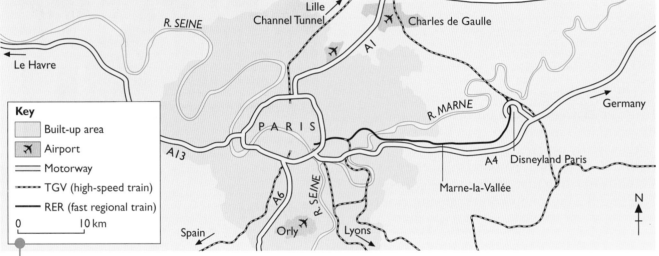

B The location of Disneyland, Paris

Activities

1 Look at map B, which shows the location of Disneyland, Paris. Describe how you could get there from Britain by:
   a) Road
   b) Rail
   c) Air.
   Use map A on page 110 to help you.

2 Write four sentences to explain how Paris meets each of the requirements of the Disney Corporation for a site in Europe.

3 When Disney was looking for a European site, it also considered London.
   Imagine that you are employed by Ile-de-France to attract new companies to the region. Compare the advantages that Paris and London offer as a site for Disney. How would you persuade Disney that Paris is a better choice?

The Disney Corporation required several things from a site in Europe:
- A large local population
- A large area of land available for development
- A place that was already popular with tourists
- A place that had good transport, including road, rail and air, making it easy to reach.

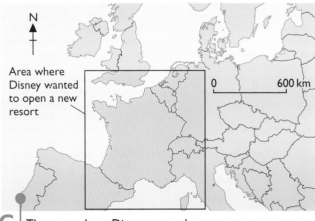

C The area where Disney wanted to open a new resort

But what is it like to live there?

> While we were in Paris, I met my pen pal, Patrick. He lives in La Villette, near the centre of Paris. I asked him what it was like to live there.

> Bonjour! I like Paris. I was born here, but lots of my friends have come from other places, some of them from other countries. Everyone comes to Paris! In La Villette there is plenty to do – swimming, rollerskating, computer clubs, and lots more. At Parc de la Villette there is even a museum of the future – the Cité des Sciences. I'm sure you would like it.

Patrick

D | Ile-de-France

Paris is the largest city in Europe. Its population has continued to grow for over 100 years. In the last few years people have been moving out from central Paris to the towns and villages around it. It's not surprising that, in many ways, Ile-de-France is the most important region in France.

	Ile-de-France (% of total)	Rest of France (% of total)
Area	2	98
Population	18	82
Professional jobs	40	60
Company headquarters	75	25

F | Population in Ile-de-France and the rest of France

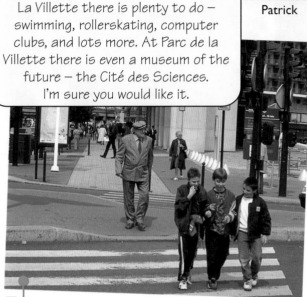

E | Part of Patrick's neighbourhood of La Villette, in Paris

Activities

1 Look at table F, which compares Ile-de-France with the rest of France. Draw graphs or diagrams to illustrate each piece of data in the table. Use the data to explain the importance of Ile-de-France to the whole of France. How do you think people in other parts of France may feel about this?

2 Look at table G, which shows how the population of Ile-de-France has changed. On a copy of the table, work out the total population of Ile-de-France for each year shown.

   Draw a line graph like the one below. Complete the two lines in different colours, using the data from the table. Draw a third line in another colour to show the total population of Ile-de-France. Label each line.

   Describe what the graph shows about changes in Ile-de-France's population.

	Central Paris population (millions)	Rest of Ile-de-France population (millions)	Total Ile-de-France population (millions)
1950	2.8	6.9	
1960	2.8	7.3	
1970	2.6	7.9	
1980	2.2	8.7	
1990	2.1	8.7	

G | Population change in Ile-de-France

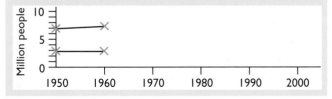

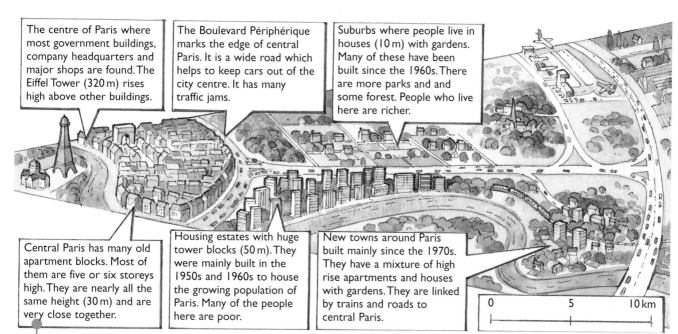

The centre of Paris where most government buildings, company headquarters and major shops are found. The Eiffel Tower (320 m) rises high above other buildings.

The Boulevard Périphérique marks the edge of central Paris. It is a wide road which helps to keep cars out of the city centre. It has many traffic jams.

Suburbs where people live in houses (10 m) with gardens. Many of these have been built since the 1960s. There are more parks and and some forest. People who live here are richer.

Central Paris has many old apartment blocks. Most of them are five or six storeys high. They are nearly all the same height (30 m) and are very close together.

Housing estates with huge tower blocks (50 m). They were mainly built in the 1950s and 1960s to house the growing population of Paris. Many of the people here are poor.

New towns around Paris built mainly since the 1970s. They have a mixture of high rise apartments and houses with gardens. They are linked by trains and roads to central Paris.

0   5   10 km

H Paris – centre to outskirts

Like other city regions, one of the greatest problems in Ile-de-France is transport. As the population has grown, more people travel to the centre of Paris every day. High-speed RER trains now link with the Metro to make journey times shorter. Despite this, many people prefer to use their cars. Almost three million cars drive into Paris every day, even though there are less than one million parking spaces! This leads to terrible congestion on the roads, especially on the Boulevard Périphérique. A new motorway ring is being built further from the centre of Paris to keep more cars out of the city.

3 Draw a cross-section of Ile-de-France to show the areas that you would pass through as you travel out from the centre of Paris. Use drawing H to help you.

Draw two scales – a horizontal scale to show the distance from the centre, and a vertical scale to show the height of the buildings.

I Inner Paris

Assignment

Imagine that your family is going to move to Ile-de-France because your mum or dad has a new job in Paris.

Study all the information in this section. Think about the differences between living in a city centre and a new town. List the advantages and disadvantages of living near the centre of Paris in an area like La Villette, and in one of the new towns like Marne-la-Vallée. Decide where you would prefer to live.

Some of my friends have moved from La Villette to other towns in Ile-de-France. I'd rather be in Paris.

J Cergy-Pontoise, a new town west of Paris

In this Building Block you will find out about the Midi-Pyrenees region, and explain why new industries are attracted there.

6.7

The Midi-Pyrenees – a quiet corner of France?

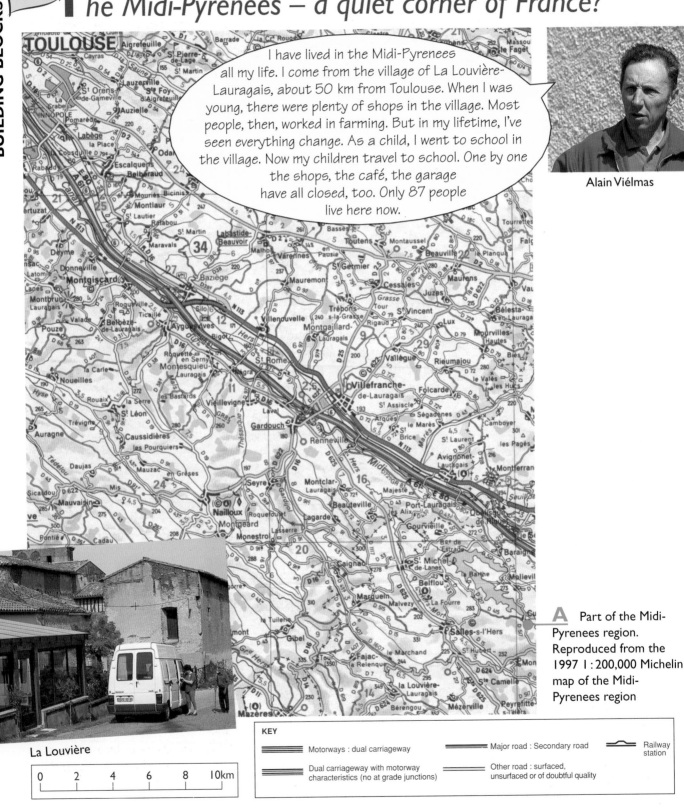

> I have lived in the Midi-Pyrenees all my life. I come from the village of La Louvière-Lauragais, about 50 km from Toulouse. When I was young, there were plenty of shops in the village. Most people, then, worked in farming. But in my lifetime, I've seen everything change. As a child, I went to school in the village. Now my children travel to school. One by one the shops, the café, the garage have all closed, too. Only 87 people live here now.

Alain Viélmas

A Part of the Midi-Pyrenees region. Reproduced from the 1997 1 : 200,000 Michelin map of the Midi-Pyrenees region

La Louvière

0   2   4   6   8   10km

KEY

Motorways : dual carriageway

Dual carriageway with motorway characteristics (no at grade junctions)

Major road : Secondary road

Other road : surfaced, unsurfaced or of doubtful quality

Railway station

B | Alain's farm

My family has farmed here for generations. There was a time, not that long ago, when a quarter of the French workforce were farmers and most of the farms were smaller than they are today. Now the number of farmers is shrinking fast. Farms today have to be efficient if they are going to compete in the European Union. It is hard for small farms to make a living. It's not surprising that you hear these stories about angry French farmers blocking roads with their tractors. My children don't want to become farmers.

0   250 m   N↑

Key
- Sunflowers
- Wheat
- Grass
- Buildings
- Water
- Roads

C | A map of Alain's farm

	Today	**In 1945**
Size (hectares)	48	20
Number of workers	1	4
Number of tractors	3	1
Outputs	Wheat, sunflowers, peas	Beef, milk, maize, wheat

D | Changes on Alain's farm

Activities

1 Look at map A, which shows the area south of Toulouse, in Midi-Pyrenees. Find the village of La Louvière-Lauragais.

2 The nearest large town to La Louvière is Villefranche. Measure the distance by road. What shops or services might Alain find in Villefranche?

   The nearest city to La Louvière is Toulouse. Measure the distance by road. What other shops and services might he find here?

   Estimate how long these journeys might take.

3 Draw a simple sketch map of the area in map A. Start by showing the areas of high land and low land shaded on the map. Shade high land brown, as in this example.

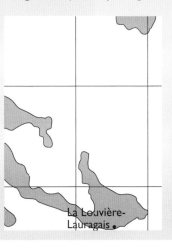

La Louvière-Lauragais •

   Mark the main settlements of Toulouse, Villefranche and Auterive, showing their size. Also mark La Louvière. Colour these.

   Draw the motorway, railway and main roads, using different symbols.

   Draw a key for your map.

4 Describe the route of the motorway and the other means of transport. Explain why they take this route. If you can find one, use an atlas map of France to find out where the motorway goes to.

5 Look at map C and table D. What do they tell you about Alain's farm? Write a paragraph to compare the farm as it was in 1945 with the farm as it is now. Use words from the box below.

   traditional   modern   livestock   mixed   arable   large   small   mechanised   unmechanised

   Explain how changes in farming and changes in the village could be linked.

   Why do you think that Alain's children do not want to farm? Can you think of any ways to make a better living from the farm?

A region of growth?

Bernadette van Accoleyen

> People in regions like the Midi-Pyrenees are turning away from traditional farming. I run a modern turkey farm and I've decided to go into tourism. I have a farmhouse that I can rent to tourists who come here. A lot of people are coming here these days for holidays.

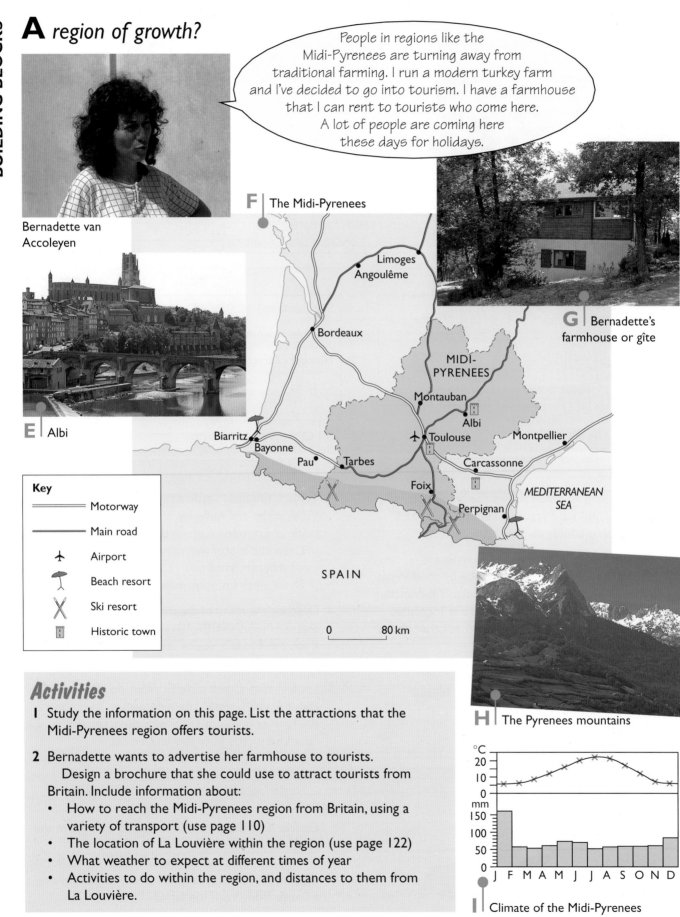

F | The Midi-Pyrenees

G | Bernadette's farmhouse or gîte

E | Albi

Key

Motorway

Main road

✈ Airport

Beach resort

✗ Ski resort

Historic town

0   80 km

SPAIN

Limoges
Angoulême
Bordeaux
MIDI-PYRENEES
Montauban
Albi
Biarritz
Bayonne
Pau
Tarbes
Toulouse
Montpellier
Carcassonne
Foix
Perpignan
MEDITERRANEAN SEA

H | The Pyrenees mountains

Activities

1 Study the information on this page. List the attractions that the Midi-Pyrenees region offers tourists.

2 Bernadette wants to advertise her farmhouse to tourists. Design a brochure that she could use to attract tourists from Britain. Include information about:
- How to reach the Midi-Pyrenees region from Britain, using a variety of transport (use page 110)
- The location of La Louvière within the region (use page 122)
- What weather to expect at different times of year
- Activities to do within the region, and distances to them from La Louvière.

I | Climate of the Midi-Pyrenees

The Midi-Pyrenees is a region that is changing. Many people now work in new manufacturing industries and services, such as tourism. Toulouse is one of the fastest-growing cities in France. It has become the centre of the French aerospace industry. It is here that large aircraft, such as Concorde and Airbus, are manufactured. Other industries have been attracted to the region, including a number of American and Japanese companies. As transport links improve, Toulouse provides a good location for industry.

K The Aerospatiale factory near Toulouse

J Toulouse

Company	Activity	Year operation began in Toulouse	Number of employees
Airbus	Aeroplanes	1995	2,300
Siemens	Electrical	1979	1,500
Motorola	Electronics	1973	3,500
Alcatel	Aerospace	1980	1,500
Aerospatiale	Aeroplanes	1970	8,500
Matra Marconi	Aerospace	1989	1,500
Electricité de France	Electrical	1969	3,000
Centre National d'Etudes Spatiale	Space research	1973	1,800

L Major industries in Toulouse

- Good, fast road network linked to the rest of France and Spain
- Warm, pleasant climate
- Cheap electricity, including hydro-electric power from the Pyrenees
- Large local market for products
- Space to build new factories
- Well-educated workforce. Toulouse has a university
- Good leisure opportunities in the region
- Airport for import and export of goods, and travel
- Large workforce from fast-growing population
- Many other large companies
- Close to Mediterranean and Atlantic ports

M Factors that attract companies to Toulouse

Activities

1 Look at table L. Describe what the data tells you about:
   a) The types of industries in Toulouse
   b) The growth of industry in Toulouse.
   Suggest why so many companies involved in similar activities should be attracted to the same location.

2 Read the list of factors in box M. Which factors could be true of many cities in France, and which only apply to Toulouse? Sort the factors into two lists.

Assignment

Draw a labelled map of the Midi-Pyrenees to show why industry is attracted to the region.

Map F shows features that attracts tourists to the Midi-Pyrenees. Would the same factors be important to attract industry? Decide which features you would include on your map, and which you would omit. Can you think of any others?

On your map, label each feature that would attract industry.

6.8

How does Ile-de-France compare...

Ile-de-France is one of the smallest regions in France, but it is, arguably, the most important. At the centre of the region is Paris, the capital city of France. It lies to the north of the country in a lowland area, known as the Paris Basin, which is drained by the River Seine and its tributaries. The climate is warm in summer and cool in winter, with fairly low rainfall throughout the year.

The region has a large population and a high population density, centred on Paris. The surrounding land is good for farming, but much of it is now urbanised.

Nearly all jobs are in either manufacturing or service industries. People and jobs are still attracted to Paris, but more of these are now moving to new towns in the region.

This is Ile-de-France, the region where I live.

A

B Climate of Ile-de-France

DATA FILE

ILE-DE-FRANCE

Size

MIDI-PYRENEES

Ile-de-France

Population

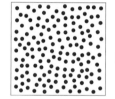
10.8

Population density

88 peop /km

Wealth per person

161% of European average

Employment

P
S
T

Unemployment

8%

C Comparision of Ile-de-France and Midi-Pyrenees

Activities

1 Study the information on these two pages, to compare the regions of Ile-de-France and the Midi-Pyrenees. To work out the size of each region, trace the grid, place it over each region on the map of France in the data file, and count the squares covered by each region.

ICT You could do further research on France, using the Internet or a CD-Rom Atlas on a computer.

2 Make a large copy of the table on the right. Complete the table, using the data file and other information on these two pages.

		Ile-de-France	Midi-Pyrenees
AREA	km²		
CLIMATE	July temp °C		
	Jan temp °C		
	Rainfall mm		
POPULATION DENSITY	km²		
EMPLOY-MENT	Primary		
	Secondary		
	Tertiary		
	Unemployed		
WEALTH	% European average		

... with the Midi-Pyrenees region?

The Midi-Pyrenees is the largest region in France. It is in the south of the country, next to the border with Spain. In the south of the region lie the Pyrenees and to the north-east is the Massif Central. Between the two mountain areas is the valley of the Garonne River, flowing to the north-west. The climate is hot in the summer and mild in winter, with fairly low rainfall through the year.

Toulouse is the largest city in the region and its population is growing fast. There are some other towns, but the region has a low population density. Much of the land is used for farming and the steeper slopes for forestry. Compared to other regions of France, a large number of people work in farming, but this is falling and more people are working in new manufacturing and service industries.

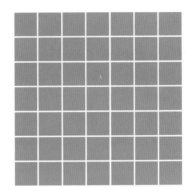

Each square on the grid is 10,000 km²

Midi-Pyrenees

2.5 m

53 people/km²

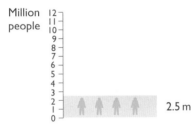

93% of European average

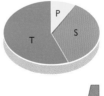

9%

This is the Midi-Pyrenees, the region where I live.

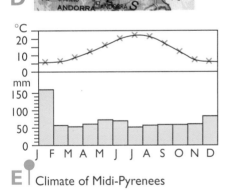

D

°C

E Climate of Midi-Pyrenees

3 The European Union gives money to regions in Europe to help them overcome their problems. Most money goes to poorer regions to help develop new industries and provide jobs to improve the quality of life. These are usually regions which have:

- Low population density, made worse by people leaving
- Few towns or cities to act as centres of industrial growth
- High unemployment
- A large proportion of people working in agriculture
- Poor transport facilities.

Decide which of the two regions, Ile-de-France or the Midi-Pyrenees, the EU would be more likely to give money to. Give reasons for your decision.

Suggest how the money could be used in that region to improve the quality of life for people living there.

Assignment

Write an article for a geographical magazine comparing these two regions. Divide your article into paragraphs to discuss:

a) The physical geography of the regions (landscape and climate)

b) The human geography of the regions (population, settlements and employment)

c) Problems of the regions.

French connections

France, like Britain, once ruled over a large **empire**, which extended across most parts of the world. Many of its **colonies** were gained during the 19th century when the countries of Europe dominated the world. Their colonies provided countries like France with natural resources, such as food and minerals, which enabled them to become even more wealthy.

The influence of France can still be seen today from the number of French-speaking countries in different parts of the world. Many of these countries became independent during the 20th century, but the French language, and other aspects of French culture, remain. A few places have not achieved independence and are still French Overseas Territories or, in some cases, Overseas Departments (each region of France is also divided into departments). The departments are still governed from Paris.

A | French colonialists in a west African village in 1900

B A sign today in French Tunisia

C | French-speaking countries around the world

N

France

Guadeloupe

Martinique

French Guiana

French Polynesian Islands

New Caledonia

Réunion

Key

Overseas departments and territories

Other French-speaking countries

Activities

1 Find a world map in your atlas. Name the French-speaking countries that are now independent, which you can see on map C. Find maps of these countries in your atlas. What do you notice about some of the place names in these countries?

2 Read the modern newspaper headlines here. What do they tell you about some of the countries that were once French colonies?

Pacific islanders blame health problems on French nuclear tests

Algerian terrorist bomb causes chaos in Paris

People in Congo refuse to speak French

Poverty in Africa worse now than 1960s

Suggest what effect colonialism might have had on countries in Africa and other parts of the world.

Homework

3 Britain, too, ruled over a large empire. Use an old atlas or history textbook to find out which countries were part of the British Empire. Use newspaper or TV reports to find out more about some of these countries today.

Since 1945, millions of people have **migrated** to Europe from other parts of the world. Many of them came to France from countries that were once its colonies. They came to find work, to escape war or persecution and for a better quality of life.

Between the 1950s and the early 1970s there was a large demand in France for people to do unskilled work, often jobs that French people did not want to do. France actively recruited people, usually men, particularly from North Africa. **Migrants** also came from neighbouring southern European countries, the Middle East and other parts of Africa. Britain experienced a similar period of **immigration** at this time.

After 1973, the oil crisis in Europe led to the growth of unemployment. France no longer had a demand for unskilled labour. People began to see immigrants as a threat to their own jobs. France,

along with other countries in Europe, imposed new immigration laws to control the number of new arrivals. Further immigration was restricted to the families of those people who were already living in France. As families were re-united a new generation of children was born in France to immigrant parents.

Since the early 1990s there has been growth in the number of **refugees** coming to Europe, often escaping wars in eastern Europe or Africa. Other people come as illegal immigrants, seeking work and a better quality of life. In France, they are likely to head for the largest cities, such as Paris or Marseilles, where the largest black and migrant populations are found.

D Migrant workers in Paris

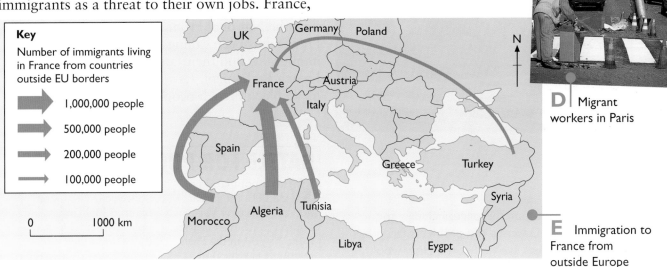

E Immigration to France from outside Europe

Activities

1 Look at map E. List the countries from which people have migrated to France. Use the map to find out how many people came from each area.
   Suggest why people migrated from these countries to France.

2 Migration happens because of **push factors** and **pull factors**. Push factors are things that make people leave their own home, like wars. Pull factors are things that attract them to their destination, like jobs. Make two lists, showing the push factors and pull factors that brought immigrants to France.

3 Read the following statement from a French government spokesperson.

'You can have a policy of stopping immigration, but you won't really stop it. The border is a door that you open and close, but it is always porous. When people are hungry for freedom and hungry to eat there's nothing you can do. Europe is like a great beacon in the night and all the birds of the night will come to it. What we have to do – through development aid – is to make the beacon shine in a much greater circle. Then the birds will stay where they are.'

Explain what you think the statement means.

Suggest what the French government could do to reduce illegal immigration.

The end of a dream?

La France est très sympathique? Je ne sais pas.

F Val-Fourré

The families of black and North African immigrants in France are often among the most **disadvantaged** section of the population. They have some of the highest rates of unemployment and live in some of the poorest quality housing in France. Many of them live on the **outskirts** (or *banlieues*) of the major cities. These are areas from which more affluent people have moved out, leaving concentrations of ethnic minority and unemployed people. Designed in the 1950s, they have a poor-quality environment, lack basic facilities, like shops, and may have poor transport links to other parts of the city. Young people in these areas are often bored and disillusioned – some turn to drugs and crime. In some cases their anger has exploded in riots, like the one described in the newspaper report in extract G. At the same time the National Front, a racist political party in France, has been calling for the repatriation of immigrants and their families. It has seats in the French Parliament. Its views are only likely to make black French people feel even more angry.

G

BATTLE FOR POOR 'BANLIEUES'

With a population of 28,000, the public housing complex Val-Fourré, in Mantes-la-Jolie, is the biggest in the Paris region. It is typical of a poor French suburb, with tower blocks built in the 1960s to house immigrant workers for the nearby factories of Renault and Simca. More than half the families are foreign, mainly from North Africa, and more than half live on state support. Unemployment is two points above the national level at 12%, but it rises to more than 20% for school-leavers.

Val-Fourré became the symbol of the crisis in the *banlieues* in May and June 1991. The centre of the complex was sacked by rioters after a youth of Arab origin died in a police cell. Then, one night in June, a policewoman was run down and killed while trying to arrest a group of joyriders, one of whom was shot dead by police a few hours later.

Today, Val-Fourré bears surprisingly few scars. The blocks of flats, recently refurbished by the state, appear in good repair. Dozens of windows sport satellite dishes, bought to pick up television from Morocco and Algeria. But a shopping centre that was brand new before the 1991 riots sits empty and looted. A crèche and day centre, destroyed in 1991, is also empty.

Extract from the *Guardian* newspaper, 15 March 1993

Activity

Read the information on this page, including the newspaper article. Describe the problems faced by young people in areas like Val-Fourré. How would you feel if you lived there?

Assignment

Work in a small group.

Imagine that you are a TV crew sent to investigate the problems of a large estate after a riot has happened. Prepare a list of questions you would ask.

Role play interviews with each of the following people:

- A young black person who has lived there since birth
- An older Moroccan person who came to France in the 1960s
- An older white French person who has recently left the area
- A spokesperson for the French government, who is responsible for housing and urban problems.

Glossary

accessible – easy to get to

agriculture – farming (growing crops and rearing animals)

air mass – a large body of air that forms over a continent or ocean

air pressure – the weight of air on the ground beneath it

arable farm – a farm that only grows crops

arch – a natural opening through a rock

atlas – a book of maps

atmosphere – the layer of air around the Earth

backwash – water running back down a beach

bay – an area of sea between two headlands

beach – material the sea deposits on the coast

bedrock – hard rock that underlies soil

biological weathering – the breakdown of rocks by plants and animals

cave – a hollow worn out of a rock

chemical weathering – the breakdown of rocks by chemical action

cliff – a very steep, rocky slope

climate – the pattern of weather over a long time

coastline – the line between land and sea marked by high tide

cold front – a line where cold air pushes under warm air, causing heavy rain

colony – an area of land occupied and governed by another country

comparison goods – things that we buy occasionally at the shops

condensation – the process of water vapour turning into water droplets

conservationist – a person who protects the environment

conurbation – a large urban area formed where settlements have merged

convenience goods – things that we buy often at the shops

croft – a small farm, usually found in remote areas

crop rotation – changing crops from one field to another on a farm in different years

dairy farm – a farm that keeps cattle for milk

defensive town – a town built on a site which can be defended

deposition – the process of laying down material to form new land

depression – a moving area of low pressure, which usually brings rain

direction – the way you are facing, shown by the points of the compass

disadvantaged – a group of people who lack opportunities

dispersed settlement – buildings spread out over a wide area

distribution – the way in which something is spread over an area, or map

diversification – increasing the variety, for example of farming activities

economic activity – industry, or the way people earn their living

empire – the colonies ruled by one country

environment – the surroundings in which people, plants or animals live

environmental quality – a measure of how pleasant the environment is

Equator – an imaginary line that goes around the middle of the Earth

erosion – the process by which rocks are worn away

European Union – a group of countries in Europe with a single market for goods

evaporation – the process of water turning to water vapour by warming

export – to sell goods to another country

extensive farming – farming over a wide area using few inputs

fold mountain – a mountain formed by the movement of the Earth's crust lifting the rock

food mountain/food lake – food surplus kept in storage

food shortage – a lack of food compared with what is needed

food surplus – an excess of food over what is needed

function – the main activity or purpose, for example of a town

geology – the study of rocks

globe – a sphere, or three-dimensional model of the Earth

grid – a pattern of squares formed by horizontal and vertical lines

grid square – a square on a map formed by grid lines

groundwater – water stored below ground in rocks

groyne – a barrier built out into the sea to slow movement of material along a beach

habitat – a place where animals or plants live

hamlet – a very small settlement without services

hard engineering – building artificial structures, for example to protect the coast

headland – land that juts out into the sea

high-order goods – things that we buy occasionally at the shops

hill farm – a farm, which usually raises animals, in a hilly area

human geography – the study of the way people live in the world

humus – decayed organic (plant) material in soil

immigration – moving to a new country with the intention of settling in it

GLOSSARY

import – to buy goods from another country
industrial town – a town that has grown around a manufacturing industry
industry – an economic activity, or type of work
input – something that is put into a system, or industry, to make it work
intensive farming – farming on a small area using many inputs
interdependence – mutual dependence of countries on each other
isobar – a line on a weather map joining places with equal air pressure

key – a list that explains the symbols on a map

landform – a natural feature of the landscape
latitude – the position on the globe north or south of the Equator
linear settlement – buildings in a line, usually in a valley or along a road
livestock farm – a farm that only raises animals
longitude – the position on the globe east or west of the Greenwich Meridian
longshore drift – the movement of material along the coast
lowest bridging point – the furthest place downstream on a river where a bridge can be built
low-order goods – things that we buy often at the shops

Maastricht Treaty – the agreement by EU countries in 1993 to closer union
manufacturing – secondary industry (making products from natural resources)
map – a drawing of a place from above, at a reduced scale
market garden – a small farm that only grows fruit and/or vegetables
market town – a town that originally grew around a market, where people bought and sold goods
Meteorological Office – the organisation that forecasts weather in Britain
meteorologist – a person who studies the weather
migrant – a person who migrates
migration – movement of people from one place or country to another
mixed farm – a farm that grows crops and raises animals

natural resources – something that can be grown, found in the sea, or dug from the ground
new town – a town designed and built recently (mainly since 1944)
nucleated settlement – buildings grouped together

occluded front – the line where a cold front catches a warm front
organic farming – farming using natural inputs, without chemicals
output – product (something that comes out of a system)
outskirts – suburbs (the area near the edge of a settlement)

physical geography – the study of the natural world
physical weathering – the breakdown of rock by changes of temperature
plan – a detailed map of a small area
plateau – a large, flat area of high land
population – the people who live in a place
population density – the number of people in an area, as a measure of how crowded it is
port – a place where ships load and unload, and the settlement around it
precipitation – rain, drizzle, snow, sleet or hail
prevailing wind – the direction the wind usually comes from
primary industry – the way natural resources are obtained from the land or sea
process – the way something happens
profit – the difference between the value of inputs and of outputs
pull factor – things that attract people to a place
push factor – things that make people leave a place

quality of life – a description of how good or bad life is for people

radial – a circular pattern with lines coming out from the centre
rain shadow – the side of a hill, sheltered from the wind, where less rain falls
refugees – people who flee their homes, usually because of war or famine
region – part of a country with its own physical or human characteristics
relief rainfall – rain caused by air being forced up, over hills and mountains
resort – a town where people go for holidays
rural – of or in the countryside

scale – a way of showing how small a map is compared with real life
scale line – a line on a map that shows how far distances are in real life
sea wall – a barrier built behind a beach to protect the coast from the sea
secondary industry – manufacturing (making products from natural resources)
sedimentary rock – rock formed from material laid down millions of years ago at the bottom of seas and lakes
service – tertiary industry (activities that meet people's needs but produce no end-product)
set-aside – land that farmers are paid not to farm
settlement – a place where people live
shanty town – an area of a city where people make their own homes
site – a place to build on
soft engineering – adapting natural processes, for example to protect the coast
soil – a thin layer of loose material on the Earth in which plants grow

spit – an extended beach that grows by deposition across a bay or river mouth

stack – a pillar of rock that stands in the sea

subsidy – money given to industries by a government, helping them to survive or improve

suburban – mainly residential area near the edge of a city

swash – the movement of water up a beach after a wave breaks

symbol – a sign used on a map

temperate – not extreme, neither very hot nor very cold

temperature – a measurement of heat

tertiary industry – services (activities that meet people's needs but produce no end-product)

trade – buying and selling goods

transpiration – the process of water in plants turning to water vapour

transportation – the movement of material by water, ice or wind

unemployment – when there are not enough jobs for every person to work

urban – of or in a built-up area

visibility – the distance through the air that you can see

warm front – a line where warm air rises over cold air, giving prolonged rain

water cycle – the movement of water between the sea, land and air

water store – a place where water is stored in the water cycle

water transfer – the way that water moves in the water cycle

water vapour – water in the form of an invisible gas

wave – circular motion of water caused by wind

weather – the condition of the atmosphere from day to day

weathering – the breakdown of rocks

weather station – a collection of instruments used to record the weather

yield – the amount of crops or animals output from an area of land

Index